Studies in Childhood and Youth

Series Editors
Afua Twum-Danso Imoh
University of Bristol
Bristol, UK

Nigel Patrick Thomas
University of Central Lancashire
Preston, UK

Spyros Spyrou
European University Cyprus
Nicosia, Cyprus

Anandini Dar
School of Liberal Studies
BML Munjal University
Haryana, India

Interested in submitting a proposal to this series? The series is co-managed by Jessica Faecks (jessica.faecks@palgrave.com) and Eliana Rangel (eliana.rangel@palgrave-usa.com). For sociological research, please get in touch with Jessica (jessica.faecks@palgrave.com), Editor for Sociology APAC and Childhood, Youth and Family Studies globally. For educational research, please get in touch with Eliana (eliana.rangel@palgrave-usa.com), Editor for Education and Youth.

This well-established series embraces global and multi-disciplinary scholarship on childhood and youth as social, historical, cultural and material phenomena. With the rapid expansion of childhood and youth studies in recent decades, the series encourages diverse and emerging theoretical and methodological approaches. We welcome proposals which explore the diversities and complexities of children's and young people's lives and which address gaps in the current literature relating to childhoods and youth in space, place and time. We are particularly keen to encourage writing that advances theory or that engages with contemporary global challenges from a critical perspective. *Studies in Childhood and Youth* will be of interest to students and scholars in a range of areas, including Childhood Studies, Children's Rights Studies, Youth Studies, Sociology, Anthropology, Geography, Politics, Psychology, Education, Health, Social Work and Social Policy.

Indexed in Scopus.

Acknowledgement

The author would like to acknowledge the support of all the people who have supported the development of this monograph:

- My interest in this topic was prompted by the bravery of one student, 'Peter', who had the courage to share a part of his story and lived experience with me. He caused me to think about how the support we offer to our students needs to change.
- Without schools willing to participate in my study I would have no data, and so I would like to thank the safeguarding teams across the country who were willing to support my work.
- For the boys who participated and shared their thoughts and occasional 'interesting' drawings, I give the biggest thank you. I consider the fact that teenagers would share such personal information with a complete stranger is an honour and one that I take very seriously.
- The supervisory team at Newman University, Karima, Roger, and Pete, who supported me with persistence and patience deserve more than the thanks I can give them.
- Finally, to my wife Alison, who has had to put up with much over the years, from questionnaires all over the tabletop whilst I entered the data into my spreadsheet, to me endlessly talking to her about my findings and especially for her interest in a topic that is so far away from her field of interest and expertise.

I would like to list everyone else by name but obviously I am unable to do this, but if you know me and I have ever pestered you or bored you with my obsessions—thank you for your friendship, support, and encouragement.

Contents

1. **Introduction**   1
   Definition of Sexting   2
   Typology   3
   References   8

2. **Theory and Practice**   11
   Introduction   12
   Digital Communication   13
   Sexting Within a Conceptual Framework   14
   Sexting and the Motivational Determinants Model   17
   References   20

3. **Adolescent Development and Sexting**   23
   Sexual Agency   25
   Sexual Identity   27
   Psychosocial Development   29
   Social Cognitive Development   33
   Associated Benefits and Risk   36
   References   42

4. **Research Methodology**   47
   School Engagement   51
   References   52

5	**Demographic and Cultural Determinants**	53
	First Exposure to Sexting	54
	Sexting Rates	54
	Sexting Content	56
	Passive Sexting	56
	Active Sexting	57
	Response to Sexting Content	57
	Sexting and the Influence of Pornography	59
	Faith and Sexting	63
	Relationships and Active Sexting by Faith Group	68
	Relationships, Sexual Identity, and Active Sexting	69
	Sexting and Ethnicity	70
	Ethnicity, Relationships, and Active Sexting	70
	School Designation, Relationships, and Active Sexting	71
	Chapter Summary	73
	References	74
6	**Determinant Cognitive and Intimate Characteristics**	77
	Gender, Sexual Identity, and Sexting	78
	Sexting and Sexual Identity	83
	Sexting and Intimate Relationships	88
	Relationships and Active Sexting	89
	Chapter Summary	91
	References	91
7	**Flirting and Social Status**	95
	The Motivation to Sext	96
	Sexual Expression as a Motivation	97
	Participant Voices Against Sexting	114
	Chapter Summary	115
	References	116
8	**General Discussion, Conclusions, and Developments**	119
	Curriculum Development	121
	Hypotheses Directing Behaviour	124
	General Summary	132
	Research Limitations	133
	Comprehension of the Legal Age to Sext	134
	References	136

9	**Recommendations for Educational Settings**	139
	Typologies	140
	Recommendations	148
	Final Words	152
	Declaration	154
	References	155

References 157

Index 169

List of Figures

Fig. 2.1	Motivational determinants model	18
Fig. 5.1	Active sexting by age	55
Fig. 5.2	Active sexting by faith	68
Fig. 6.1	Active sexting by relationship status	90
Fig. 7.1	Reason for sexting by motivational category	97
Fig. 7.2	Motivational category: sexual purpose	98
Fig. 7.3	Motivation: Body image and recipient status	103
Fig. 7.4	Image content	104
Fig. 7.5	Motivation: As a joke by age	109
Fig. 7.6	Motivation: To feel wanted	111
Fig. 7.7	Motivation: Aggravated factors	114
Fig. 9.1	Four motivation options typology model for boys	147

CHAPTER 1

Introduction

Abstract The rise of digital communication has spotlighted sexting as a form of adolescent sexual expression, though its definition remains fluid. While often seen as the exchange of self-generated, sexually explicit images, sexting can also include suggestive texts, AI-generated content, and explicit drawings. Broader interpretations encompass consensual, contextual, and non-consensual content, shaped by social norms around gender and sexuality. Understanding male sexting behaviour requires examining diverse motivations, ranging from relationship dynamics, humour, and body positivity to peer belonging and harassment. This book focuses on boys aged 14–18, viewing sexting as a potentially normative part of adolescent development. It adopts an individualised approach, avoiding generalisations about teenage behaviour. Crucially, it excludes coercive or adult-involved sexting, instead focusing on consensual, peer-based practices. By doing so, it aims to better understand how sexting fits into the sexual and social growth of teenage boys in a digital age.

Keywords Active sexting • Boys' experiences • Cultural determinants • Defining sexting • Experimental sexting • Passive sexting • On-line interaction

© The Author(s), under exclusive license to Springer Nature Switzerland AG 2025
J. Needham, *Addressing Sexting in Educational Spaces*, Studies in Childhood and Youth,
https://doi.org/10.1007/978-3-031-96398-8_1

Definition of Sexting

With the increased use of communication technology have come reports of 'sexting' as an expression of teenage sexuality (Van Dijke et al., 2025). However, what is shown from the literature is that a clear description of this practice does not exist. In its simplest form, 'sexting' is a portmanteau of the words 'sex' and 'text' and represents sending and receiving of sexual content. However, Del Ray et al. (2019) identify that sexting definitions vary depending on the type of content being sent as either sexually explicit or erotic. Therefore, a definition of sexting needs to accept any potential descriptive conceptual limitations and classify a range of practices. The definition could identify sexting as exclusively sending self-generated, sexually explicit images and films or encompass a wider set of behaviours to include the sending and receiving of both sexually explicit and suggestive photographs, text messages, videos and artificial intelligence (AI) generated images, and explicit line drawings such as the manga cartoon sub-category of *Yaoi* or *Hentai* artwork via digital media platforms and mobile communication devices.

Reed et al. (2020) caution that a simple definition of sexting is not easily arrived at and argue that classification must also identify subsets against which behaviours can be mapped. Van Dijke et al. (2025) develop this further by reporting a shift in academic classification of sexting behaviours to adopt a more categorical means to look at sexting behaviour. The authors identify four descriptive categories: by dividing sexting behaviour into 'active' and 'passive' forms of sexting. The active role in sending sexts or the passive action of receiving or being asked to send a sext. The second category highlights consent as a central concept in sexting interactions and divides sexting behaviour into 'consensual' and 'non-consensual' sexting. The third category distinguishes between primary and secondary sexting. Primary sexting refers to sexting behaviour that occurs in a relationship between the person who sends a self-produced sext and the person who receives that sext, and secondary sexting is everything that takes place outside of this primary relationship such as the forwarding of sexts. The last category is described in the Wolak and Finkelhor (2011) typology model that identifies malicious, coercive, criminal, and abusive elements within 'aggravated sexting', and 'experimental sexting', which occurs in the context of a romantic liaison, attention seeking, or similar behaviours.

Dolev-Cohen (2024) and Van Dijke et al. (2025) all argue that without a clear definition of sexting practice then the response by professionals will be compromised by various colloquial uses. Clarity in the definition and content of messages with clearly defined, rather than ambiguous descriptions of content will facilitate understanding and intervention. Courtice and Shaughnessy (2017, p. 270) refer to sexting characteristics across all the possible forms holistically as technology-mediated sexual interaction to include 'any interpersonal interaction that includes self-created, sexually explicit content e.g., creating and exchanging videos, or messages and occurs through the use of digital technology'. The most accurate definition of sexting then is, by necessity, the more complex definition. This definition must reflect the wider range of behavioural traits, images, along with a review of the explicit nature of the content. Therefore, a description of sexting needs to consider the role of 'active' sender or 'passive' recipient, and the inclusion of explicit text, images, pseudo-images, self-generated media, and links to pornographic content creation within social media sites.

Typology

Few research publications discuss the definition of sexting with young people themselves. Albury (2015) in a research group with young men and women described two groups of images, 'Private or Public Selfies'. They identified that regardless of the level of explicit content, it is the intention behind the picture that defines its categorisation. Private selfies are not created to be shared, but for the owner to reflect on oneself, either as a sexual being, or to measure physical appearance and muscular definition. Public selfies were framed by the young people as an unremarkable, albeit potentially risky, practice designed to aid communication and an expression of 'self' that communicated interests and desires to their peers. In addition, Setty (2019a, 2019b) reported teenagers, especially young men, saw sexting as a normal activity and also expected of them within sub-cultures of society, either those in which hegemonic masculinities are the norm that reinforce a self-confidence and pride in their bodies, or by the adults that interact with them on a professional basis anticipating the curation of images and distribution of images.

Albury (2015) presented this broad typology of images that included private and public selfies but also identified other definitions: contextual images of situations where a state of semi-undress was considered normal e.g., at the beach, joke images, inoffensive sexual images shared consensually between peers or partners and offensive and unethical sexual pictures that included images shared without consent. Paasonen et al. (2019) argue that self-generated explicit images are subject to degrees of semantic flexibility not only about whether they are indecent or risky in terms of reputational damage, but also that the desirability of the image is linked to the social norms connected with gender, sexuality, and sociability. In attempting to frame the motivation behind the sending of a picture of a penis to others, Waling and Pym (2017) propose four reasons: Firstly, because males do not understand what women want; secondly because men find and attribute humour and playfulness with the penis; thirdly as a means of expressing body positivity; and finally, to intimidate and harass others.

The 2020 United Kingdom Council for Child and Internet Safety (UKCIS) who provide guidance for educational spaces within the UK describe sexting only as 'sending nudes' and identify two main categories of 'nude' based upon the study by Wolak and Finkelhor (2011). This typology was developed after examining the criminal intent behind sexting after reviewing cases of explicit imagery that had come to the attention of the US legal system. This model identifies incidents within an 'experimental' modality; youth generated images and circulated to another young person to further romance, fun, or entertainment, and 'aggravated' images created with malicious intent e.g., created in exchange for money or gifts, forced by someone, exacerbated by peer pressure, or to hurt or damage another. The UKCIS guidance then directs schools to address experimental incidents in-house or for aggravated episodes by referral to the police.

However, Sesar et al. (2019) argue that the motivation to sext is influenced by contextual variables that need to be considered within a broader typology model. They argue that these variables include intimate relationship dynamics, flirting or the desire to gain intimacy in relationship, demographic identifiers such as age, sex, gender, and cognitive influences such as personal attitudes towards sexting, perception of self-image, social status, and peer pressure. These variables will all have an impact on motivation and so need to be considered when classifying sexting.

UK law, through the On-line Safety Bill (2022), reminds professionals that regardless of the philosophical or sociological stance taken, the legislation around sexting remains clear, that particularly the sharing of naked images of children under 18 years old remains illegal. The introduction of formal warnings and the decisions made not to criminalise teenagers has lessened the likelihood of indictable action when images are shared willingly between minors. This allows the 'normalised' teenage behaviour, as described by Davidson (2014, p. 104) as 'just one of the many adaptations sexual expressions has made to new technology' leading to the production of self-produced sexual images to be reviewed separately from the making, possession, and distribution of illegal images of child abuse.

The published research and lived experience of the young people within schools makes it clear that sexting does occur and appears to be embedded within the youth sub-culture. Therefore, it is necessary to challenge the essentialist arguments that sexting is always harmful and linked to risk (Morelli et al., 2021; Dolev-Cohen, 2024). Understanding the nature, perceptions, beliefs, and cultures that underpin a teenager's motivation to act will allow strategic direction, through policy design based on actual practice.

This book aims to identify the motivating factors and the behaviours exhibited by boys; the underpinning theoretical framework needs to consider the individual rather than teenagers' as a generalised homogeneous group. However, this book will not explore sexting practice that is undertaken as an act of coercion or control, or behaviours that involve those over the age of 18 years, or where there is an intention to harm. These potentially exploitative behaviours would support a protectionist milieu and would fall within a definition of aggravated sexting. Rather, this book will solely focus on sexting practice in boys aged 14–18 years, within the domain of experimental sexting between peers and may be interpreted as a normal demonstration of teenage sexual behaviour.

Within the published research, the act of sending an electronic sexualised message is often portrayed as a technological, legal, and moral crisis. With the panic focused on girls and sexting, who are often depicted as at risk of sexual commodification and are held to greater account for their participation in sexting (Symons et al., 2018). This book will attempt to address the perceived gendered double standard surrounding sexting; where the common narrative focuses primarily on the impact sexting has on girls as victims and boys as perpetrators. Anastassiou (2017) develops this theme by identifying that research generally defines sexting where girls are identified as either victims or promiscuous. However, the sexting behaviours and the impact on boys as potential victims, other than occasionally because of their sexual orientation, or the motivational factors that prompt sexting in boys, are rarely examined in the literature. Sexting is presented as normalised and acceptable behaviour, often classed as a joke.

Models of sexual citizenship based on the traditionally accepted standards of hegemonic heterosexual masculinity legitimise a hierarchy that subordinates other expressions of masculinity. This can lead to the endorsement of sexual double standards that can restrict a man's emotional response, openness and responsiveness within a relationship, and can present a duality between their own sexual experience and the expectations placed upon them within their social group. Ricciardelli and Adorjan (2018, p. 570 and p. 572) describe this discounting of males' emotional responses as 'culturally emasculating' and 'trivializes male experiences thus forcing boys to suffer in silence or risk violating the norms of socialised masculinities'. Clarke et al. (2018) note that for young men that identify as gay, bisexual, transgender, or a gender identity other than heterosexual, the societal normative assumption further underestimates their response and supports the call from Ricciardelli and Adorjan (2018, p. 577), criticising responses to sexting that are 'based on individual responses to atomistic circumstances instead of a broader sociological topography of digital sexual expression'. This is not to detract from the important recognition that pressure or coercion or problematic practices occur as factors within some sexting practice.

Adopting a solely positivist approach to solve the 'problem' of sexting would not support the response to the individual circumstances of each young person, which requires a phenomenological interpretation to understand their situation. It is important then to find an approach to deliver support that allows a response to the individual but also identify a broader field of learning within a wider population and signpost to corresponding behaviours. To address the individual circumstances of each young person requires a degree of interpretivism into the enquiry so that it can recognise the importance of the individual constructions alongside clear legal and policy directives. Therefore, this book is not about identifying an idiographic response to the 'truth' as experienced within a participant's individual situation, rather, it is to adopt a nomothetic approach that involves different sub-sets of boys with the purpose of discovering the general principles or 'truths' that characterise the influencing factors and motivations to sext amongst boys in general. It is important that any understanding around this topic gathers the voice of the participant rather than solely that of the professional.

The axiological basis for this book is to provide a voice to young people, whose values are often overlooked, and to ensure that their needs and preferences are reflected in decision-making and development of policy. One of the fundamental principles of axiology as an ethical value, in the rational feature of estimative intentionality, is that every human being has intrinsic value and worth. Values guide human behaviour and decision-making, influencing how people perceive and respond to their environment and play a crucial role in shaping people's lives and the world around them (Velázquez, 2023). By trying to understand the different value systems inherent in each young man and the reasons behind them, it is hoped to identify the underlying motivations and reasons that support their choices in their sexting behaviours.

Providing a voice to this population group is important because their values are often marginalized or ignored in society and therefore limit their opportunities to participate in decision-making processes, which can further exacerbate their marginalization. Similarly, young people's values are often overlooked because of the assumption that they lack the experience or knowledge to make meaningful contributions. However, young people are important stakeholders in society, and their values and preferences should be considered in processes that affect their lives. Moreover, given the speed of change within technology, young people often have unique perspectives, which can contribute to innovative solutions and sustainable development and can empower them and enhance their sense of agency. Young people's voices are often silenced or ignored; instead their voices should be heard. They have their own experiences, thoughts, and feelings, and they should have a say in matters that affect them. Therefore, this book aims to examine 'value' from a participant perspective, within the general, rather than a focus on moral or ethical values, to emphasize the plurality and heterogeneity of the boys' experiences within the motivational factors expressed. This resistant design approach aims to highlight the voices of those teenage boys who engage in sexting and ensure that they are properly represented, to ensure that alternative voices are not subsumed by an unquestioning adherence to the dominant 'harm' discourse.

This book will examine the theoretical background to sexting as well as the experiences of young people in practice to understand the motivating factors that influence sexting behaviours of teenage boys by examining six hypotheses:

1. The older the boy the more likely they are to sext.
2. The prevalence of sexting varies with the boy's ethnicity.
3. Boys who identify as other than heterosexual are more likely to sext.
4. Boys who regularly access porn are more likely to sext compared against the behaviours of their peers.
5. Boys in a relationship are more likely to sext.
6. Boys with an active faith are less likely to sext.

Exploring these determinants will enable educational settings to understand the contextual issues within sexting practice and address them though clearly defined policy and practice.

REFERENCES

Albury, K. (2015). Selfies, sexts, and sneaky hats: Young people's understandings of gendered practices of self-representation. *International Journal of Communication, 9*, 1734–1745.

Anastassiou, A. (2017). Sexting and young people: A review of the qualitative literature. *The Qualitative Report, 22*(8), 2231–2239.

Clarke, K., Cover, R., & Aggleton, P. (2018). Sex and ambivalence: LGBTQ youth negotiating sexual feelings, desires, and attractions. *Journal of LGBT Youth*, published online, June, 1–16.

Courtice, E., & Shaughnessy, K. (2017). Technology-mediated sexual interaction and relationships: A systematic review of the literature. *Sexual and Relationship Therapy, 32*(3–4), 269–290.

Davidson, J. (2014). *Sexting gender and teens*. Sense Publications.

Del Ray, R., Ojeda, M., Cassas, J., Mora-Merchán, J., & Elipe, P. (2019). Sexting among adolescents: The emotional impact and influence of the need for popularity. *Frontiers in Psychology, 10*(1828), 1–11.

Dolev-Cohen, M. (2024). Patterns of sexting by youths: A latent class analysis. *Journal of Sex & Marital Therapy, 50*(6), 679–690.

Morelli, M., Urbini, F., Bianchi, D., Baiocco, R., Cattelino, E., Laghi, F., Sorokowski, P., Misiak, M., Dziekan, M., Hudson, H., Marshall, A., Nguyen, T., Mark, L., Kopecky, K., Szotkowski, R., Van Demirtaş, E., Outsel, J., Voiskounsky, A., Bogacheva, N., Ioannou, M., Synott, J., Tzani-Pepelasi, K., Balakrishnan, V., Okumu, M., Small, E., Nikolova, S., Drouin, M., & Chirumbolo, A. (2021). The relationship between dark triad personality traits and sexting behaviours among adolescents and young adults across 11 countries. *International Journal of Environmental Research and Public Health, 18*(2526), 1–25.

Paasonen, S. Light, B., & Jarrett, K. (2019). The dic pic: Harassment, curation, and desire. *Social Media and Society*, April–June, 1–10.

Reed, L., Boyer, M., Meskunas, H., Tolman, R., & Ward, M. (2020). How do adolescents experience sexting in dating relationships? Motivations to sext and responses to sexting requests from dating partners. *Children and Youth Services Review, 109*(104696), 1–10.

Ricciardelli, R., & Adorjan, M. (2018). If a girl's photo gets sent around, that's a way bigger deal than if a guy's photo gets sent around: Gender, sexting, and the teenage years. *Journal of Gender Studies, 28*(5), 563–577.

Sesar, K., Dodja, A., & Šimić, N. (2019). Motivational determinants of sexting: Towards a model of integrating the research. *Psihologijske Teme, 28*(3), 461–482.

Setty, E. (2019a). 'Confident' and 'hot' or 'desperate' and 'cowardly'? Meanings of young men's sexting practices in youth sexting culture. *Journal of Youth Studies*, Published on-line, July, 1–17.

Setty, E. (2019b). A rights-based approach to youth sexting: Challenging risk, shame, and the denial of rights to bodily and sexual expression within youth digital sexual culture. *International Journal of Bullying Prevention*, Published on-line, November 19, 1–14.

Symons, K., Ponnet, K., Walrave, M., & Heirman, W. (2018). Sexting scripts in adolescent relationships: Is sexting becoming the norm? *New Media & Society, 20*(10), 3839–3857.

Van Dijke, S., Van den Eynde, S., & Enzlin, P. (2025). The bright side of sexting: A scoping review on its benefits. *Computers in Human Behavior, 164*, 108499. https://doi.org/10.1016/j.chb.2024.108499

Velázquez, J. (2023). Feeling in values: Axiological and emotional intentionality as living structure of ethical life, regarding Max Scheler's phenomenology. *Human Studies, 46*, 43–57.

Waling, A., & Pym, T. (2017). C'mon, no one wants a dic pic: Exploring the cultural framings of the dic pic in contemporary online publics. *Journal of Gender Studies, 28*, 70.

Wolak, J., & Finkelhor, D. (2011). *Sexting: A typology*. Crimes against Children Research Center. Published on-line, November, 1–16.

CHAPTER 2

Theory and Practice

Abstract The integration of emerging technologies into education has reshaped teaching and policy, posing challenges for educators, especially in supporting vulnerable youth whose digital and real-world experiences increasingly overlap. As digital platforms become central to learning, teachers are expected to manage students' on-line sexual behaviours, despite differing perceptions of technology use. This chapter explores adolescent sexting through the lens of the Theory of Reasoned Action, focusing on attitudes, subjective norms, and perceived behavioural control. These elements influence how boys perceive sexting outcomes, respond to peer and societal pressures, and assess their ability to engage or abstain. Adolescent development, marked by physical, emotional, and social changes adds complexity to sexting behaviours. Understanding sexting within this developmental and motivational framework allows for a nuanced, individualised analysis. This approach helps educators and policymakers move beyond disciplinary responses, recognising sexting as a developmental phenomenon shaped by intention, context, and technological interaction.

Keywords Adolescent sexting • Body image • Digital communication • Faith and sexting • Flirting • Gender identity • Individual determinants • Motivation to sext • Subjective norms

Introduction

To understand the motivation that prompts sexting activity, it is first necessary to identify a conceptual framework to illustrate the issues faced in the prevalence of adolescent male sexting. In the examination of the motivating factors that prompt the teenage boy's sexting habits it will lead to an understanding of teenage boys' actions and help to define a typology that will enable a more effective response to address behaviour through specifically designed curricular and pastoral support.

The epistemological concepts and ontological response around sexting behaviours are constantly emerging as digital mobile technology and geospatial applications develop and social mores change, whilst the national law regulating any activity and public opinion lags. In the United Kingdom (UK), as in many other countries, whilst the age of legal majority is assumed at 18 years old, the age of consent to sexual activity is 16 years old. However, images involved in sexting are dealt in UK law through the Protection of Children Act 1978 and the Criminal Justice Act 2008. The production, sharing, distribution, and storage of explicit images of those under 18 years old are dealt with as child abuse, with a similar legislative stance being taken in other countries' legal systems. Because the making of, the distribution and storage of explicit images are dealt with as abuse, participation cannot be consensual under the existing legislation. The On-line Safety Bill (Great Britain. Parliament. House of Commons (2022)) received royal assent in October 2023 and promotes the offence of 'sending a photograph or film of genitals' where a person (A) intentionally sends or gives a photograph or film of any person's genitals to another person (B) will have committed an offence, if (a) A intends that B will see the genitals and be caused alarm, distress, or humiliation, or (b) A sends or gives such a photograph or film for the purpose of obtaining sexual gratification and is reckless as to whether B will be caused alarm, distress, or humiliation. The On-line Safety Bill does not specify a definition of age for this new offense, or for the age of the victim. Phippen and Bond (2023, p. 95) argue that the proposed legislation rather than 'calling for a change in the law to support victims and bring the legislation in line with protections for adult victims of the nonconsensual sharing of images', instead implies that social media 'service providers "have the technology" to detect and prevent the transmission of an intimate image by a minor'.

DIGITAL COMMUNICATION

The statutory guidance regulating the management of sexting incidences for teenagers under the age of 18 years is unclear with only a loose distinction made between the consensual and non-consensual sharing of nude and semi-nude images and/or videos referred to as youth produced sexual imagery and the acknowledgement that 'consensual image sharing, especially between older children of the same age, may require a different response. It might not be abusive, but children still need to know it is illegal, whilst non-consensual is illegal and abusive' (Great Britain. Department for Education, *Keeping Children Safe in Education*, footnote 8, 2024). Whilst government guidance also specifically excludes instruction on how to deal with graphically sexual written communications (UK Council for Internet Safety, 2020, p. 5), instead referring practitioners to local policy that may vary dependent on a particular individual or agency stance.

From pedagogy to policy development, teaching practice to curriculum implementation, all aspects of education have been affected by the application of emergent technology. The increased availability of digital network spaces presents a new challenge for educational professionals meeting the needs of young people they consider to be vulnerable, where their 'online' world spills into the 'real-world' day. For schools this is increasingly pertinent where the increased use of digital technology is relied on in the classroom (Livingstone & Smith, 2014). Ryan et al. (2014) identify an issue with teachers being expected to police the boundaries of sexual behaviour and acceptable actions. The perception, purpose, and use of digital technologies by adolescents and teachers vary in use for creative opportunity, developmental understanding, and proficiency. Placing the responsibility on the schoolteacher to moderate the digital environment in school requires the professional to view technology both as a liability and an asset when addressing the issues around teenage agentic sexual behaviours.

A United Kingdom YouGov Survey (2019) of smartphone or mobile phone access or ownership by teenagers aged between 14 years to 17 years in 2019 recorded a median percentage of ownership at 96.5%. In a similar 2022 study of smartphone ownership penetration in the UK for young people aged 16 years to 24, the figure rose from 86% in 2018 to 99% in 2022 (Statista Survey, 2023) clearly demonstrating that mobile phone technology is integrated into teenage life.

Davidson (2014) and Sheilds Dobson and Ringrose (2016) propose that there is a strong relationship between the development of what they describe as the adolescent curriculum of sexuality and the growing development of sexual communication within digital platforms. This link was further proposed by Holoyda et al. (2018) who write of the impact on adolescent development (including the formation of sexual agency) that increased access to on-line communication methods can have. Their research on young people's behaviours and underlying motivation to engage in sexting identified that adolescents use mobile technologies as a way of exploring sexuality, gender identity, and levels of intimacy.

Sexting Within a Conceptual Framework

Ajzen et al. (1982) reasoned that to understand why a person acts in the way they do, it is important to understand the attitude that prompts that behaviour. This 'theory of reasoned action' argues that to understand a behaviour, it is necessary to understand the intention. Ajzen et al proposed that the attitude towards the behaviour and the societal context in which the actions take place, which they refer to as the Subjective Norm, are affected by the weighting placed by the actor against the relative importance they hold on to that specific behaviour.

This approach appreciates that whilst subjective norms differ between individuals and vary across ages and can be subject to differing cultural interpretations, intention can only predict behaviour if these subjective factors do not change between intention and behaviour. That being, where behaviour is proportionally linked to intention, when considered against the individual's attitudes and subjective norms.

Ajzen recognised within an individual's situation people have incomplete volitional control over behaviours, and that the aggregation of behaviours across occasions and situations allowed for a better model of measuring the underlying behavioural disposition rather than an individual behaviour. The Theory of Planned Behaviour (Ajzen, 2011) acknowledges that behavioural control will change depending on the situation and actions undertaken by the individual. This includes what the participants themselves feel are factors that influence their behaviour, the source of that influencing factor, and their confidence in their ability to perform the behaviour. Ajzen argues that the personal attitude towards a behaviour is directly proportionate to the expectancy value of the participant's salient beliefs and the personal evaluation of the subjective norms. This model implies that the attitude towards a behaviour is proportionate to the participant's belief structure and evaluation of normative influences.

If this conceptual model is applied to that of sexting behaviour it would postulate that a relationship exists between a teenage boy's belief about a behaviour, i.e. that sexting is permissible and beneficial, his attitude towards that behaviour, i.e. that sexting does not cause harm, and his perception that sexting is seen as 'normal' in popular youth culture. Therefore, if a teenage boy is engaged in consensual sexting with a romantic partner, this would be represented as the likelihood to sext is directly proportional to the belief that it causes no harm, and everyone else is doing it and would then be seen as a justification and endorsement of his behaviour and actions.

However, Ajzen's Theory of Planned Behaviour does not define what would constitute the attitude, subjective norm, or perceived behaviour control. Dolev-Cohen (2024) suggests that subjective norms are a strong predictor of intention to engage in sexting and applied this model to their study into sexting and identified that, where teenagers viewed sexting as a form of technology-assisted flirting that their attitude towards sexting was positive and therefore were more likely to participate in the behaviour. Those that associated it with a range of negative outcomes were less likely to be involved in sexting practice. In their study, the adolescent dependence on the importance of their peer group as a key reference point and the need for conformity with this group provided the Planned Behaviour subjective norm. Validation by association with their peer group, to respond to the social pressure to sext, was seen as a motivating factor to participate. Finally, Walrave et al identified that the perceived behavioural control was split into two key factors: the first being the availability of the technology to participate in sexting and the second the impact of 'significant others' in their lives and their attitude towards sexting. Their study showed in response to the first behavioural control that teenagers had both the means of access to mobile phones and the technical skills required to participate in sexting. In the second that the attitude of their peers had more impact as a behavioural control than those of trusted adults such as a parent, teacher, or religious leader.

Factors within current youth culture, the physical and psychological development that function as influencing factors and would make up the subjective norm that have an impact on the participants' attitudes toward sexting. These factors were considered as the basis for a definition for the formation of attitudinal belief, of the subjective norm, and have an impact as a behavioural control measure.

Adolescent development is a complex and critical phase marked by physical, cognitive, emotional, and social changes that significantly influence behaviour. Understanding the framework that sexting sits within allows the understanding and analysis of the factors driving adolescent boys' sexting behaviour in the context of their developmental stage.

Relating a motivational framework to sexting, then attitudes refer to how adolescent boys perceive the positive or negative outcomes of engaging in sexting. Subjective norms encompass the influence of their peers, parents, and the societal expectations on an adolescent's decision to sext. Perceived behavioural control relates to an adolescent's perception of their ability to engage in or abstain from sexting.

If adolescence is a period of heightened susceptibility to social influences, where fitting in and seeking approval from peers become paramount. This developmental characteristic interacts with sexting behaviour through subjective norms. Peer pressure and the desire to conform to perceived norms around sexting can significantly impact an adolescent's decision to engage in such behaviour. Similarly, attitudes play a crucial role as adolescents weigh the perceived benefits of sexting, such as enhancing their social status or relationships, against the potential risks, such as privacy breaches or reputational damage.

Perceived behavioural control is especially relevant in the context of adolescent development. Adolescents often experience a sense of invincibility, leading them to underestimate the potential for negative consequences. This overestimation of control might contribute to risk taking behaviours including sexting, especially if they believe they can control who sees the content and prevent any negative outcomes. However, whilst these identified factors may influence sexting behaviours, they, in and of themselves will not describe the motivation behind the young person's actions, and so the theory of planned behaviour only partially offers a solution. Sesar et al. (2019) designed an approach that, whilst still based in the theory of social learning from which grew Ajzen's work, developed a model to explain the motivational determinants for participating in sexting.

In this alternative model, the individual determinants retain a positive correlation with Ajzen's 'subjective norms' but allow for idiographic interpretation of the factors influencing an individual rather than a more general nomothetic view, in relation to this study, of all teenagers and as a homogenised group. The Motivational Determinants model proposed offers further insight by emphasising the importance of motivational factors in driving behaviours. This model identifies the motivational dimensions of seeking pleasure and dominance as relevant when examining adolescent sexting behaviour.

Seeking pleasure aligns with the curiosity and exploration characteristics of adolescence, the allure of excitement and novelty can drive boys to engage in sexting, especially as they navigate their emerging sexual identities. Seeking dominance ties into the power dynamics that can be inherent in sexting exchanges; adolescents might engage in sexting to assert their desirability or control over others, reflecting the developmental need for autonomy and self-assertion.

Whilst the teenage brain structures are still developing, particularly in areas related to decision-making and impulse control, the lack of full cognitive maturation can lead to an underestimation of the potential legal and social consequences of sexting, aligning with the avoidance of punishment dimension. Additionally, the tendency to prioritize short-term rewards over long-term consequences can be seen as adolescents avoiding the effort required to consider the potential risks associated with sexting.

Sexting and the Motivational Determinants Model

The interaction between adolescent development, focusing on sexting behaviour, and the importance of developing a comprehensive understanding of the factors influencing adolescent sexting must be identified. The role of attitudes, subjective norms, and perceived behavioural control in shaping intentions to sext within the Theory of Planned Behaviour amplifies the impact of subjective norms; however, it identifies further the need to understand the motivations involved. The Motivational Determinants model developed by Sesar et al. (2019) adds depth by exploring how motivations contribute to sexting behaviour. By addressing attitudes, social norms, perceived control, and underlying motivational factors, researchers, educators, and policymakers can work together to empower adolescents to make informed decisions aligned with their overall well-being.

Alongside the impact of demographic characteristics, the Motivational Determinants model examines the understanding of sexting by the participant in their agreement to sext. The model is built on the assumption that cognitive understanding leads to a participation in sexting, and that positive reactions to a sexting event are the strongest determinant to continued behaviours. However, the model does not account for the potential for unconscious motivation and the affective as opposed to the cognitive dimension and this limitation is acknowledged.

In the same way that Ajzen saw perceived behaviour controls as modifying factors in behaviour prediction, Sesar et al. (2019) report the potential for contextual determinants to influence the motivation to sext. The development of the work by Sesar et al is rooted in the understanding that sexting is an exclusively delinquent style behaviour that generates within its participants the desire to participate in other risk-taking behaviours and seek out other delinquent individuals. Sesar's model is situated in a protectionist approach around delinquent, risk-taking behaviour, and the second, places sexting as a developmental expression of 'usualised' behaviour, i.e. it is now a widespread practice among young people to engage in technologically assisted sexual expression.

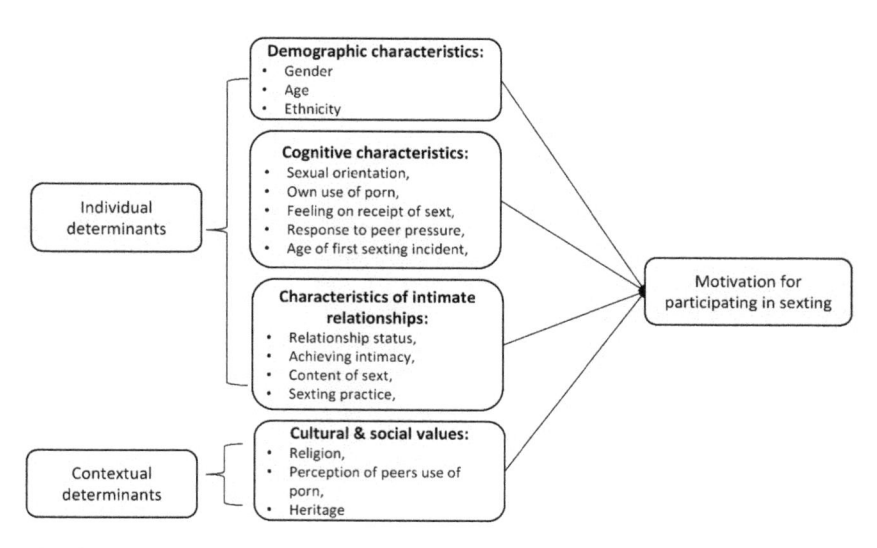

Within the Motivational Determinants model (Fig. 2.1), the demographic profile of the participants, the cognitive characteristics of sexual orientation, relationship status, use of pornography, and the cultural and societal values placed on the expression of faith and religious attitudes towards sexting behaviours were used as a map to determine the characteristics of sexting as an intimate act and to provide a theoretical model to analyse the motivational characteristics data.

Individual determinants
- **Demographic characteristics:**
  - Gender
  - Age
  - Ethnicity
- **Cognitive characteristics:**
  - Sexual orientation,
  - Own use of porn,
  - Feeling on receipt of sext,
  - Response to peer pressure,
  - Age of first sexting incident,
- **Characteristics of intimate relationships:**
  - Relationship status,
  - Achieving intimacy,
  - Content of sext,
  - Sexting practice,

Contextual determinants
- **Cultural & social values:**
  - Religion,
  - Perception of peers use of porn,
  - Heritage

→ **Motivation for participating in sexting**

Fig. 2.1 Motivational determinants model

Reed et al. (2020) identified a motivational factor for sexting is for boys to seek peer feedback about the adequacy of their body. This was reinforced by Needham (2021) whose study identified reports of sexting to show muscular definition or as a means of boasting. Albury (2017) identified that some images posted by boys were an attempt to show muscle definition and could be posted on social media sites as an attempt to gain 'likes'. Burén and Lunde (2018) write of the impact of sexting on the perception of self on body image and body dissatisfaction and function as a tool by which adolescents explore and express sexuality and as a measure of moderation and integration in their friendship groups.

The lines of demarcation between the motivational options should not be seen as singular or absolute, rather as covariant. Obtaining approval for body shape and image could be a precursor to flirting with a partner to initiate sex or a relationship. The sending of images to a friend or group of peers could be an expression of identity, create a sense of social cohesion or a form of behavioural reinforcement around a traditionally accepted view of masculinity.

The motivation to sext, to explore identity and social status is one that has received much attention. The notion of sexting to maintain the masculine hegemony is explored by Garcia-Gómez (2019, p. 316) in his discussion of 'the relational and communal layers of the self' to establish an identity based on characteristics thought to be 'normal' for the boy in question, but also how he wishes to be seen by those significant in his life and by his peers.

This construction of and exploration of identity is also reflected in work by Bianchi et al. (2019) who write of teenagers' need to conform to perceived behavioural norms in their peer group. Ojeda et al. (2019, p. 108) writes that 'by taking part in sexting, boys boost their social prestige and gain popularity in their peer group', whilst the opposite is noted for girls. Setty (2019a, 2019b, p. 9) noted that some instances of sexting were perceived as 'jokes and banter' and that the social construct of masculinity was reinforced when images shared between male friends focused on what they 'look like' in terms of body shape and penile or callipygian aestheticism rather than the focus on the fact they have shared a naked image. Paasonen et al. (2019, p. 6) define a sociocultural context where the 'curated dick pic', a naked picture, is shared by heterosexual or homosexual men with other men as a potential for community and kinship without attaching any meaning of sexual identity or purpose; that the 'penis in particular, remained the key focus of attention and curatorial effort'. This was noted especially in young men who identified as gay or non-binary (Needham, 2021; Van Ouytsel & Dhoest, 2021), who describe the sharing of naked images as a way of gaining acceptance into what they perceived as the gay community.

REFERENCES

Ajzen, I. (2011). The theory of planned behaviour: Reactions and reflections. *Psychology & Health, 26*(9), 1113–1127.

Ajzen, I., Timko, C., & White, J. (1982). Self-monitoring and the attitude-behaviour relation. *Journal of Personality & Social Psychology, 42*(3), 426–435.

Albury, K. (2017). Just because it's public doesn't mean it's any of your business: Adults' and children's sexual rights in digitally mediated spaces. *New Media & Society, 19*(5), 713–725.

Bianchi, D. Morelli, M. Baioco, R. Chirumbolo, A. (2019). Individual Differences and developmental trends in sexting motivations. *Current Psychology* Published on-line.

Burén, J., & Lunde, C. (2018). Sexting among adolescents: A nuanced and gendered online challenge for young people. *Computers in Human Behavior, 85*, 210–217.

Davidson, J. (2014). *Sexting gender and teens*. Sense Publications.

Dolev-Cohen, M. (2024). Patterns of sexting by youths: A latent class analysis. *Journal of Sex & Marital Therapy, 50*(6), 679–690.

García-Gómez, A. (2019). Sexting and hegemonic masculinity: Interrogating male sexual agency. In P. Bou-Franch & B. Garecés-Conejos (Eds.), *Empowerment and Dominant Gendered Norms: New Insights and Future Directions* (pp. 313–339). Analyzing Digital Discourse.

Great Britain. Parliament. House of Commons. (2022). *On-line safety bill*. The Stationary Office.

Great Britain. Department for Education. (2024). *Keeping children safe in education*. The Stationary Office.

Holoyda, B., Landess, J., Sorrentino, R., & Hatters-Friedman, S. (2018). Trouble at teens fingertips: Youth sexting and the law. *Behavioural Science Law, 36*, 170–181.

Livingstone, S., & Smith, P. (2014). Annual research review: Harms experienced by child users of online and mobile technologies: The nature, prevalence, and management of sexual and aggressive risks in the digital age. *Journal of Child Psychology and Psychiatry, 55*(6), 635–654.

Needham, J. (2021). Sending nudes: Intent and risk associated with 'sexting' as understood by gay adolescent boys. *Sexuality & Culture, 5*(2), 396–416.

Ojeda, M., Del Rey, R., Ortega-Ruiz, R., & Casas, J. (2019). Sexting: A new way to explore sexuality. In F. Wright (Ed.), *Digital technology* (pp. 99–124). Nova Science.

Paasonen, S. Light, B., & Jarrett, K. (2019). The dic pic: Harassment, curation, and desire. *Social Media and Society*, April–June, 1–10.

Phippen, A., & Bond, E., 2023. A progressive future?. In *Policing teen sexting: Supporting children's rights while applying the law* (pp. 93–114). Springer International Publishing.

Reed, L., Boyer, M., Meskunas, H., Tolman, R., & Ward, M. (2020). How do adolescents experience sexting in dating relationships? Motivations to sext and responses to sexting requests from dating partners. *Children and Youth Services Review, 109*(104696), 1–10.

Ryan, G., Schubert, A., & Wurf, G. (2014). Adolescent setting in schools: Criminalisation, policy imperatives, and duty of care. *Issues in Educational Research, 24*(2), 190–211.

Sesar, K., Dodja, A., & Šimić, N. (2019). Motivational determinants of sexting: Towards a model of integrating the research. *Psihologijske Teme, 28*(3), 461–482.

Setty, E. (2019a). 'Confident' and 'hot' or 'desperate' and 'cowardly'? Meanings of young men's sexting practices in youth sexting culture. *Journal of Youth Studies*, Published on-line, July, 1–17.

Setty, E. (2019b). A rights-based approach to youth sexting: Challenging risk, shame, and the denial of rights to bodily and sexual expression within youth digital sexual culture. *International Journal of Bullying Prevention,* Published on-line, November 19, 1–14.

Sheilds Dobson, A., & Ringrose, J. (2016). Sext education: Pedagogies of sex, gender, and shame in schoolyards of tagged and exposed. *Sex Education: Sexuality, Society & Learning, 6*(1), 8–21.

UK Council for Internet Safety. (2020). Sharing nudes and semi-nudes Advice for education settings working with children and young people Responding to incidents and safeguarding children and young people. UK Council for Internet Safety.

Van Ouytsel, J., & Dhoest, A. (2021). The prevalence, context, and perceptions of sexting among non-heterosexual men from various generations in Belgium. *Computers in Human Behavior, 126*. Published on-line.

CHAPTER 3

Adolescent Development and Sexting

Abstract This chapter examines sexting within the context of adolescent psychosocial and social cognitive development, focusing on how it relates to sexual agency and gender identity in teenage boys. While adolescence is a universal biological phase, its meaning varies culturally; in Western societies, it is shaped by delayed adulthood, formal education, and digital access, which foster identity exploration. The chapter critiques early androcentric theories and instead promotes a multifactorial approach that integrates biological, cognitive, and psychosocial factors. Puberty and brain development influence self-perception, emotional regulation, and risk-taking—key elements in sexting behaviour. Using a developmental framework, the chapter explores how attitudes, subjective norms, and perceived behavioural control shape sexting decisions. It also evaluates the potential risks and benefits of sexting, emphasising the importance of context and intention. Ultimately, it advocates for a culturally sensitive, developmentally informed understanding of sexting that supports adolescent growth in increasingly digital social environments.

Keywords Adolescent risk-taking • Biological development • Cultural relativism • Experimental sexting • Group identity • Impulsivity • Motivation • Peer influence • Risk-taking behaviour

© The Author(s), under exclusive license to Springer Nature Switzerland AG 2025
J. Needham, *Addressing Sexting in Educational Spaces*, Studies in Childhood and Youth,
https://doi.org/10.1007/978-3-031-96398-8_3

The concept of adolescence, as it is commonly understood today, is often regarded as a western construct rooted in cultural, historical, and socio-economic factors. Whilst the teenage years, as a biological stage in human development is universal, its interpretation, significance, and the challenges associated with it are subject to cultural and contextual variations (Yunkaporta & Shillingsworth, 2020). It is necessary to explore the concepts of adolescence through cultural relativism, by examining the biological, psycho-social influences on teenage boys, and the implications of this perspective on sexting behaviours primarily through a western construct.

A western understanding of adolescence is deeply influenced by socio-cultural factors, including formal education systems and a delayed entry into the workforce. Alongside this is the exploration of identity and independence and an increased access to technology. An ethnocentric approach to adolescence can overlook the diversity of adolescent experiences in different cultural contexts of a multi-cultural society and can perpetuate a narrow and ageist view of youth and the contributions young people can make to their community. Adolescents in western societies are encouraged to question authority, make independent decisions, and pursue personal goals. These values contribute to the perception of adolescence as a distinct and formative life stage.

It is argued by Ojeda et al. (2019, p. 102) that despite the evolving concepts around sexting, it remains vital to establish an objective stance which is unproblematic and can be seen as a 'clear, validated and universal definition, which can lay the foundation for our knowledge'. The development of an idiographic definition of sexting that considers the intention of the message either as aggravated or experimental in nature and to delineate between sexual content and exposure linked to the developing gender identity and behaviours over time, as opposed to one that represents the vicissitudes of social change and moral decline.

The aim of this chapter then, is to identify the academic background to the phenomenon of sexting by establishing how the sending of explicit, self-generated images and messages sits within the development of adolescent sexual agency and gender identity based within relevant theories of psychosocial and social cognitive development. Finally, this chapter will examine if sexting can be associated with benefits or risks to the adolescent.

Sexual Agency

The theoretical construct of adolescence is difficult to define within the literature due to the shifting focus of research and methodological approaches. The domains of social psychology, cognitive psychology, and developmental neuroscience each present theories that explore the development of the teenager. Kolano (2013) writes that whilst every teenager experiences an individual response to the biological, social, hormonal, and cultural changes that occur in growth and maturation, the theories of psychosocial development view teenagers as a group and underestimate the variability of individual experience.

If sexting is viewed as a precursor to sexual activity, then the influence of pubertal development and particularly the increase of sex hormones need to be investigated as a causal factor in sexting initiation rates. Pingle et al. (2017) identified that a concomitant causal link can be made between increasing testosterone levels, thorarche, the development of secondary sexual characteristics, and the motivation to engage in sexual activity. They report that whilst gender variation exists in sexual behaviours, hormonal changes, peer influence, and social context are predictors of the initiation of sexual behaviour in females, but that in males, physiological development was the main determinant for sexualised behaviour.

The sexual motivation system of adolescent neurodevelopment is dependent on hypothalamic-pituitary regulation, reflexive sexual behaviour, and the hippocampal comparator matching function of subjective satisfaction or pleasure and is dimorphic in its presentation (Hadley, 1989). Steinberg (2010) notes that the pre-frontal cortex area of the brain, responsible for executive functioning, matures at a much slower rate than the cortical features of the amygdala and the hippocampus in the paralimbic areas. This blurring of the developmental stages between limbic and paralimbic regions and the frontal cortex are responsible for an emotional, rather than a logical response in teenage behaviour. Pingle et al. (2017) report a positive correlation between risky sexual behaviours and brain responses in the inferior frontal gyrus, and changes in the left occipital gyrus during response inhibition. This finding suggests that physiological development of the adolescent brain to regulate action is in part dependent on external psychosocial factors which need to be considered when studying the stimulus and motivation in a response linked to sexual activities.

Walrave et al. (2014, p. 87) identify that intellectual capacity increases during adolescence, allowing teenagers to become capable of 'making active, informed, and responsible sexual decisions'. The mid-adolescent period is a crucial phase in the development of sexual agency, with teenagers' cognitive maturity enabling them to reflect on their sexual feelings, motivations, behaviours, and the contiguous relationship between the development of adolescents' sexuality and the growth of sexual communication within digital platforms.

Hasinoff (2015) notes that teenage sexual agency needs to be framed as relative and contextual within the wider community. Whilst the recognition of teenage sexual agency is an essential pre-requisite in the argument that consensual sexting is a 'right' that should be supported as a part of a claim to sexual citizenship. Hasinoff argues that misinformed definitions of teenage development are used to deny competence and therefore undermine agency. The argument can be made that if adolescents are not yet developed as fully rounded humans, subject to physical and neurological limitations, then they may not be ready to exercise their rights. The function of the biological or psychological immaturity argument then presents technology as a risk; that despite the desire not to misuse, teenagers just cannot help themselves. 'Adolescents are often described as irrational, impulsive, out of control and even crazy or stupid. This pejorative characterization is usually attributed to teen physiology: raging hormones, still developing brains and an innate orientation to their peers' (Hasinoff, 2015, p. 49). This leaves them in need of adult protection through the control and criminalisation of a range of risky behaviours, including sexting, until they achieve actual maturity or majority.

Setty (2019a, b) argues that the response to sexting by some professionals working with young people appears to reverse a teenager's right to privacy when dealing with the sharing of sexting incidents. They argue that the responsibility for a breach in privacy is blamed on the person sending a message, rather than the person circulating a message to others. They comment on the narrative that states the risks of sexting are well known and to avoid the wider circulation of images they should not be shared in the first instance. This argument ignores the concept of sexting within a stable and loving relationship and shifts the blame to the victim that creates 'an appealing narrative that simple common-sense rules of risk reduction can prevent on-line victimisation…regulating and controlling the potential victims' behaviour—rather than the potential assailant is often an ineffective strategy that implies sexual assault is inevitable' (Hasinoff, 2015, p. 59).

The argument that 'victims bring it upon themselves' has been refuted through the anti-rape narrative but continues to exist in educational resources where responsibility is moved from those who share received images onto the victims who failed to assure their own safety in an on-line environment. Albury (2017) argues for a fundamental shift in curriculum resources away from shaming the victim where a breach in privacy has occurred, to focusing on the person who has breached the confidentiality of the victim. Albury writes, 'What if being known as 'someone who gossips and shares sexual images without consent' was the *more* shameful identity and was presented to young people as such?' (2017, p. 722). The argument that this potential damage to reputation and employability both places the blame where it should lie and would impact on behaviours.

Sexual Identity

Lindquist et al. (2021, p. 333) write that the terms sex and gender are often used interchangeably, but that their definitions have distinct meanings. Sex refers to the biological classification assigned at birth based on chromosomes and reproductive characteristics, but they argue that an extensive definition of gender is required to operationalise effective research from a performative perspective which reflects a social construct within societal norms (Ricciardelli & Adorjan, 2018). Gender expression is identified as the characteristics that society places on roles assigned to people and is described as to the individual's self-representation as male or female and/or to socialisation based on others' interpretation of sex. Rosen et al. (2019, p. 2) further define gender identity as 'one's internal sense of feeling like a man or woman' leading to a definition of cisgender as one where the gender expression, gender identity and sexual characteristics align'. As clear definitions of gender continue to evolve, it is argued that 'gender expression exists on a continuum and may vary in definition from individual to individual' (Jacobson et al., 2015, p. 204). Clarke et al. (2018, p. 1) note that 'identity is understood as a non-voluntary performance and articulation of selfhood in accord with prevailing norms and discourses'; therefore young people are defining their gender and sexual orientation as they interpret it, as a cultural shift in the taxonomies of sexual identity.

It is argued that an attempt to quantify 'identity' introduces the concept of dualism, of 'them' and 'us', of who fits and does not fit into a defined gender or orientation. Lindquist et al. (2021, p. 336) describe the process of 'them' and 'us' as a form of 'othering', which reinforces and reproduces a form of subordination by defining who differs from the 'norm'. To reify gender identity into a simple set of categories does not fully capture the complexities of identity in all its varied and pluralised categories. McCormack (2011, p. 665) states that simplification obscures the complex nature of gender and identity, and 'limits the life experiences of sexual minorities, polices gendered behaviours, and stigmatises non-masculine youth' and through Queer Theory map homosexually themed language within research and policy. This post-structural approach sees gender identity to be open, fluid, and non-fixed and challenges the notion of categorising as heterosexual or homosexual, deconstructing both into the unicity of the individual.

Hammack and Manago (2024) note that, for lesbian, gay, bisexual, transgender, and questioning (LGBTQ+) youth, identity development involves awareness that their sexual orientation and gender identity may differ from what they perceive as society's norm. The issue of sexual identity formation can be seen as a cognitive and affective congruency between an individual's perception of self, of their behaviours, and of others. This was outlined in the theoretical model of homosexual identity formation developed by Cass (1979) where she defines six stages of identity that a person must work through to achieve identity synthesis. Her model is clear that moving between stages is individual and a personal matter that differs between people, and that identity foreclosure may mean that for some the full integration of sexuality and other aspects of self may not occur. Cass does not ascribe an age profile to the developmental stages but for most young people they will be identifying with some of the stage characteristics at around 14 or 15 years of age. Several factors influence this 'coming out' process for young people, including the perceived level of support from family and friends, the social acceptance of a gay lifestyle within their cultural identity, religious beliefs, and the ethos of the school they attend. According to Kosciw et al. (2015), identity development, and particularly disclosure, is a complex process that involves risk of victimisation and that this must be balanced against the increased resilience, higher self-esteem, improved academic performance, and the improved emotional and mental health that labelling oneself as LGBTQ+ and disclosing this to others brings.

Albury and Byron (2014) argue that much of the research into sexting practice does not distinguish between heterosexual usage and that of same sex attracted young people. They argue that this lack of recognition in current research typically 'heterosexualises' the issues and potentially adversely frames the chances taken by young people who identify as gay, bi-sexual, or gender fluid. Bauermeister et al. (2014) note that young men who identify within sexual minorities e.g., homosexual, bi-sexual, or transgender are more likely to engage in sexting behaviour and expose themselves to what would be classified as high-risk sexual practices.

Psychosocial Development

Many of the original early twentieth-century theories of adolescent development sit within an androcentric assumption that what is true for males is equally applicable to females and are based within a framework of biological maturity, behavioural theory, external environmental events, or contextualism. However, the multifactorial nature of teenage development draws together all these factors and their impact on the motivation to sext. Adolescence is seen as a critical phase of human development characterized by profound transformations in various dimensions of life. This transitional period is marked by intricate interactions between the psycho-social, social-cognitive, and biological development domains. In the context of adolescent boys, these developmental dimensions intertwine to shape their journey towards adulthood, impacting their identity formation, relationships, cognitive abilities, and physical maturation.

The interplay between psycho-social, social-cognitive, and biological development in adolescent males yields a dynamic landscape of growth, challenges, and opportunities. This complex interplay influences their identity exploration, relationships, cognitive abilities, and physical changes. Acknowledging and understanding these dimensions in relation to sexting practice is key to providing appropriate support and resources, fostering healthy development, and paving the way for a successful transition to adulthood.

The biological changes of adolescence are the most visibly apparent, with the onset of puberty marking a significant milestone. In boys, puberty is triggered by the release of testosterone, leading to the development of secondary sexual characteristics (Pingle et al., 2017). This transformation not only influences their self-perception but also impacts how adolescent males are perceived by others, potentially shaping their self-esteem and social interactions. These biological changes during adolescence extend beyond the external. The adolescent brain undergoes structural and functional reorganisation, particularly in regions responsible for impulse control, emotional regulation, and decision-making. It is argued that this ongoing neurological development can contribute to the characteristic risk-taking behaviour observed in adolescents, as they navigate newfound cognitive capacities alongside evolving emotional landscapes.

Psycho-social development during adolescence entails a series of intricate changes in emotional, psychological, and social dimensions highlighting the central challenge of identity versus role confusion. Adolescent boys undergo a process of growth and self-discovery where they explore their role and values. This search for identity is influenced by personal experiences, societal expectations, and cultural contexts.

Peer relationships take on heightened significance during adolescence. Adolescent boys seek peer acceptance and validation, leading to the formation of close friendships and the establishment of peer groups. These relationships provide opportunities for emotional support, shared experiences, and the development of interpersonal skills. Simultaneously, peer pressure can exert both positive and negative influences, impacting decision-making and behaviour.

Freud's stages of Psychosexual Development Theory argue that during the 'Genital Stage' the process of emotional detachment is shifted from the parent to a substitute and then finally to libidinal attachment within their peer group. This emotional detachment presents as a rejection or resentment to rules set by the parent, making behaviours that challenge the contextual norm more appealing. Freud argues that societal values are already imprinted on the teenage superego during the Latency Period. To control the internal and external influences of sexual development and gratification requires the erotic feelings to be sublimated into activities considered more productive such as sport rather than sexual activity.

Lichtenberg (2013) proposed in his psychodynamic framework of motivational systems that three factors develop innately in a teenager in response to basic needs: The need for the expression of sexuality between peers and sexual partners, the expression of aggression in response to situations, and the need for positive reinforcement of body image. Lichtenberg's theory outlines that, as an individual grows these motivational systems are demonstrated through on-line activity by reorganising according to needs, desires, dependent on the intrapersonal experiences and social exchanges with peers. In relation to the motivation to sext, the sending and receiving of explicit communication forms part of the innate system to expression of sexuality, intimacy, and dyadic satisfaction or to gain the affirmation required to confirm body adequacy or express an affiliation with a specific peer group.

Erikson's (e.g., 1950) 'Stages of Man' Theory of Adolescent Development similarly argues that a teenager must explore their sense of sameness and continuity to develop their identity against a period of identity confusion. He argues that unlike the development of secondary sexual characteristics, identity development is not automatic, but dependent on societal factors and psychosocial reciprocity such as the accessibility to appropriate role models. Erikson argues that during this stage of development, sexual activity, and so by definition sexting, is an attempt to define identity by the validation of self-feeling and sexual identity through the reactions of others.

Sullivan (e.g., 1953) describes this validation of sexual identity in his Heuristic Stages of Development Model. Prompted by genital maturity in the Early Adolescent Stage, the teenager experiences a discord between an Intimacy Dynamism, developing their personal identity and a Lust Dynamism; the desire to attain intimacy with another person. It is possible therefore to argue that the failure to integrate the Lust and the Intimacy Dynamisms create the opportunity for aggravated sexting, where a young man sees a member of the opposite sex, or a same sex attraction, as a person who can meet their genital needs but not their need for intimacy. Therefore, that member of the opposite sex can be subjected to unsolicited sext messages and the curation and circulation of images to others or be understood and interpreted as someone who can provide friendship, love, and support.

Fairbairn (1994) developed an approach to psychoanalysis that can see sexuality more about forming relationships rather than meeting a set of basic drives. This 'Object Relations Theory' Model proposes that impulses appear within the setting of dynamic structures that relate to an external object i.e., a person or another internal object. The progressive differentiation of the internal or external world that occurs during sexual development and may influence the sexting habits of a teenage boy. The application of Fairbairn's conceptual framework proposes that the response to a subjective object, such as an explicit image or sexualised message within a sext (as a representation of the person as the 'object'), may be an appercipient response linked to existing ideas around gender identity and sexual response, or an introjectal or imago response but not a radical division between an internal or external world event.

This psychosocial development is explored within the Theory of Cultural Conditioning where Mead (e.g., 1950) proposed a conflict between the co-figurative and pre-figurative cultural domains a teenager exists within. The traditional values enshrined within a co-figurative culture used to describe the shift from an extended family structure to a smaller nuclear family that identifies social change and the possible isolation of a young person. This can lead to a feeling of disconnection from family or authoritarian role models, who are felt as irrelevant to the dimensions of youth and therefore reject what are seen as adult mores e.g., not to sext. These dimensions represent the individual and contextual determinants that effect influence on the teenagers' development. Therefore, compared to his female peers, the slow maturing male may exist within a pre-figurative culture, which is a conception of reliance on self, rather than the guidance of others, because he is not psychologically or physically mature enough. The concern is that the pressure to conform may make the young male engage in risky behaviours or sexual intimacy which is outside of the normal developmental expectations for age.

Piaget (e.g., 1953) and Kohlberg separately argue that moral judgement and cognitive ability develop simultaneously. For a young person to develop a moral judgement and attitudinal belief structure in relation to the practice of sexting requires them to understand the difference between 'right' and 'wrong' and decide upon their personal view of the topic. Within Kohlberg's (e.g., 1963) suggested Interpersonally Normative Morality Stage, the desire to seek approval in moral development is closely aligned to the defined morality of their peer group. Kohlberg acknowledged that the development of the perception of morality differs significantly in males and females in their relationship to self and society. The argument was made by Gilligan (1977) that women address moral dilemmas differently to men and demonstrate care and responsibility more often than men. Therefore, if the perception for teenage boys is that their peers are engaging in sexting, then this becomes a powerful contextual determinant in their own attitudes and behaviour.

Selman (e.g., 1980) in his work defining the Structural-Developmental Model of Social Cognition defined adolescent thinking within five phases, Stage 0 to Stage 4. The third stage of which allowed the teenager to begin to see social interaction from multiple perspectives; how it affects them and how others might feel. This developing self-awareness allows the teenager to approach situations appreciating other perspectives and allowing resolution to conflict. Selman's final fourth stage of adolescent development takes this self-awareness further to allow the teenager to appreciate an in-depth societal perspective of situations. The understanding of another's perspective of how the mutuality with social systemic construct works depends on the adolescent being able to appreciate the consensual group perspective and consider the societal, conventional, legal, or moral perspectives involved.

Selman's model creates a link between the 'Social Systems Morality' in the Kohlberg model and synthesises the developmental growth patterns in social cognition and the developing social competence which can function as cognitive determinants towards the motivations to participate in sexting or not. This would allow the adolescent to be appreciative of the impact, both positive and negative, these sexting behaviours can have on others. Indeed, Selman further explored this in his work into verbal exchange and social behaviour in pair interaction in two dimensions. The first being the importance of asserting a sense of self over others, and the opposite of taking a submissive stance and acquiescence to another's request.

In applying Selman's theory around the strategies for interpersonal negotiation it is possible to fit the application of coercive, aggravated sexting between the level 0 Egocentric Undifferentiated and the level 1 'Will Driven' power stages. In these states, it is the desire to dominate others and meet only the personal needs that leads behaviour. Where sexting within a developing relationship could be seen to sit within the level 2 'Conscious Reciprocal Persuasion' stage that allows the acknowledgement of genuine attempts in seeking a duality of outcome, but that self-interest outweighs mutual interest. The development of mutually beneficial intimate relationships would then fit within Selman's descriptions of the level 3 'Mutual Perspective Taking' or level 4 'In-depth Social Perspective Taking' stages where people are both dependant on, and supportive of each other. This model of development acknowledges that behaviours can move between levels and the higher function requires maturity and self-reflection not common in the early teenager.

Social Cognitive Development

Cognitive development can be outlined in stages through which boys progress in their ability to think abstractly and reason logically. During this adolescent phase, cognitive abilities develop at a rapid pace, facilitating the exploration of complex concepts and the analysis of hypothetical scenarios. This cognitive growth equips boys with the capacity to engage in more advanced problem-solving and critical thinking as they move from a development driven by external rules and approval to one characterized by the development of a personal moral code based on abstract principles. This progression reflects the maturation of their ethical reasoning and contributes to the formation of their own value system.

It is argued by Muss et al. (1996) that Social Cognitive Theory proposes that, rather than a link to the defined stages of adolescent growth that individuals learn from others and this learning is the determinant of behaviour change. This means then that learning can occur at any age, and teenagers behave differently because of the social expectations placed on them, or as a reaction to social factors that assert different influences. The implications of social learning theory in relation to sexting depends then on the teenager's ability to self-regulate and reflect on the outcome of behaviours. If in the process of sexting, the youth is under the impression that everyone is doing it, and that the reward is the desired level of sexual intimacy, then the ability to regulate their behaviour will be influenced by a potentially skewed frame of reference.

This behaviouristic view is that learned responses are dependent on external reinforcement and vicarious learning from the consequences of the actions undertaken by the individual or others. In relation to sexting behaviours, if the young person sees no negative consequence to his actions or no negative response in his peers, then that behaviour will be validated. A tenet within Social Cognitive Theory is that there is a reciprocal bidirectional relationship between the individual, their behaviour, and the external social environment they function within. Therefore, whilst adolescents as a group may reject adults as identification models, the opportunity exists for a teenager to learn from the positive behaviours exhibited by an authoritarian role model whilst still rejecting the person.

Bandura (e.g., 1977) challenged the stage theory assumptions of psychosocial development, that stress, rebellion, and peer conformity define adolescence. He argues that these are behaviours linked to cultural expectation and conditioning, resulting as the consequence of antecedent conditions in child-rearing and parent-child relationships. This social learning theory postulated that environmental variables, past experiences, and exposure to different models are responsible for differences in behaviour. His argument is that operant conditioning explains how learned behaviour is maintained, but not how it is initially acquired. The theory of cognitive social learning is that patterns of behaviour are acquired through observation of behaviour performed by a role model.

In Bronfenbrenner's (e.g., 1993) Four Ecological Systems model, access to the people who can function as positive role models extends beyond the family microsystem to the social roles taken by authority figures within the mesosystem. However, confusion may occur when the microsystems the teenager lives within (i.e., family group or friendship group) hold, or endorse divergent values and the potential presents itself for peer influence to override learning from parents or responsible adults. The impact the adolescent has on the wider political and legal community which is described as the exosystemic environment is limited but may constitute an external determinant on their behaviour. The classification of sexting as an aberrant behaviour, and the threat of prosecution may affect the teenager's attitudes as a perceived behaviour control.

Phippen and Bond (2023) argue that in adopting Bronfenbrenner's ecosystem approach and applying it to on-line safety and sexting, the responsibility for intervention sits with a wider breadth of stakeholder agencies. These agencies need to share the responsibility for safeguarding young people and manage the interdependencies between them. The teenager sits at the centre of the Ecosystem model, at the centre of their microsystem, interacting with their immediate environments, both off-line and on-line. The immediate spheres which influence a child's life include the education system, law enforcement, social care, as well as their family and peer groups. These exosystemic mesosystems provide infrastructure for the child's on-line experiences and influence both their vulnerability and resilience.

One exosystemic influence can be viewed through the control measures suggested in the application of Routine Activity Theory as proposed by Mohammad and Nooraini (2021). The theory is based upon the determinant influence of three main components: Capable Guardianship, Motivation to Offend, and a person as a Target for Attention. In applying Routine Activity Theory to the issue of sexting, Holt et al. (2016) make the argument, in relation to on-line sexual conversations. The absence of a 'capable guardian' is represented through the lack of an adequate parental monitoring role model either in-person or as inadequate monitoring software. That the teenager wanting to initiate or maintain contact with a romantic association undertakes the role of the 'motivated offender', and the recipient of the active sexting message would represent the 'suitable target' so that sexting defined as a 'delinquency based behaviour' can be explained and validated.

Hill (e.g., 1980) developed the ecological perspective in the Context-Based Model of Adolescent development, based on three primary changes that mark the transition from childhood to adolescence: the biological changes within puberty and the appearance of primary and secondary sex characteristics resulting in an increase in sex drive. The social changes in the way an individual sees themselves and the expectations placed upon them by society; and the cognitive changes that allow for systematic consideration to possibility and probability and abstract reasoning. Hill reasoned that these primary changes were impacted on by cultural microsystems and the secondary changes experienced by the adolescent of identity development, sexuality, and the achievement of personal goals and choices.

Associated Benefits and Risk

Much of the published literature assumes risk as *a priori* and focuses on the dangers posed to adolescents when sexting without recognising the subjective and dynamic nature of risk or demonstrating causality between activities and outcomes. O'Sullivan (2014) noted that the reporting of incidents focuses on aggravated sexting events where images have been shared widely without consent, or on the issue of possession of child abuse images and the potential for prosecution. Lee and Crofts (2015, p. 468) write that much of the literature into sexting 'often begins with an adult orientated moral agenda that unproblematically takes sexting on board as a negative risk' and that this risk is then used as a new framework through which adolescent sexuality is managed. This is supported by Naezer (2018, p. 772) who writes that risk and arising moral panic 'mainly function to moralise about, pathologize and police particular behaviours'.

Handschuh et al. (2018) published a meta-analysis of the literature and concluded that the published research associated sexting with sexual behaviours and 'risky' sexual practice, without clearly defining what these practices were. Similarly, what is often missing from much research is any focus on risks that do not necessarily lead to negative outcomes, for example, sexting for pleasure and the positive effect within relationships. Jonsson et al. (2015, p. 1246) write that young people were aware of the possible risk associated with sexting but 'saw more benefits than risks associated with the behaviours and felt personally less vulnerable to negative consequences'. Dijke et al. (2025) argue that an approach to sexting that acknowledges the risk and benefits that can arise from sending a sexualised message is likely to be a more positive response to the issue. This builds on work by Champion and Pedersen (2015) who argue that sexting can be seen as a new mode of communication with a partner and a safer sex alternative. An example of this is seen in a study by Needham (2021) where 100% of the teen participants, who self-identified as homosexual, and who identified themselves as being in a relationship, used sexting as part of their relationship.

O'Sullivan (2014, p. 46) introduces a note of caution when examining the potential for risk and increased participation in harmful behaviours when considering sexting. She notes that 'much of the alarm and hysteria surrounding young people's participation in on-line sexual activities has been reinforced, even magnified, by the research designed to highlight both'. The argument she proposes is that technology is so embedded and integrated with modern life that going back to a pre-technology era is not possible. Rather than wishing for simpler times, O'Sullivan challenges that the use of technology should be realigned to meet specific issues through curriculum development in school and encouraging young people to modify the sexual content within their on-line profiles.

O'Sullivan also argues against the double standards portrayed in the general media noting that mainstream reality shows on television and digital media providers encourage people to share all elements of their life. She argues that the increasingly permissive sexual attitudes portrayed on these programmes encourage young people to talk openly about sex among themselves. O'Sullivan (2014, p. 47) argues that 'most young people are overall relatively savvy regarding the inherent risk associated with on-line technology use… young people seem to equate keeping something private with being ashamed of it and revealing something as having pride'. She argues that the fall in teenage pregnancy rates, increased use of contraception, and reduction in sexually transmitted diseases show that the modern-day youth are more sexually risk averse than previous generations. Phippen and Brennan (2016) proposed that young people estimate the risk they face by comparing themselves with the activities of their peers and saw more benefits to an activity than risk and felt that consequences happened to others.

Whilst many studies reference risky sexual behaviour, few clarify the meaning of risk and attempt to define which behaviour may carry more risk than another. Baumgartner et al. (2010) identified an ascending scale of risk associated with sexting from on-line conversations about sex, searching for someone to have sex with, sending explicit photographs, and meeting an on-line contact off-line to sell sex. The study identified additional risk when the contact was made with strangers. This risk was highlighted in a report by Morelli et al. (2021) and Needham (2021) who identified that young people from sexual minority groups rather than their heterosexual peers were more likely to sext with a stranger. Champion and Pedersen (2015) identified that the most notable differences in sexting practice were found in those participants who identified as bi-sexual compared to those who identified as heterosexual. The percentage of bisexual participants increased as the content of the message became more explicit compared to a slight decrease in sexting rates amongst the heterosexual participants when the content became more explicit.

These findings echo an integrative review undertaken by Van Ouytsel et al. (2015) that reported that adolescents who participate in sexting were also more likely to engage in off-line sexual behaviours. This study found that a contiguous relationship exists between an adolescent's level of sexual behaviour and the content of the explicit nature of the sext sent. That teenagers who limited their sexting to explicit messages only were less likely to engage in sexual activity that resulted in oral or vaginal sex. Korenis and Billick (2014, p. 98) note within their study that of boys aged 14–19 years old who send a sext message, 82% also reported having active sexual relationships compared to 45% who reported not sending sexually explicit messages. Champion and Pedersen (2015) note that on-line sexual activity rather than physical contact removes the risk of sexually transmitted disease and pregnancy and therefore can be viewed as a beneficial consequence of sexting. Pingle et al. (2017) write that limiting sexual activity to sexting only may be a way of delaying physical sexual activity and supporting a young person's decision to delay because of a personal principle or tenet based within the main principles of a religion or philosophy.

Weisskirch et al. (2017, p. 691) caution that there are no empirical studies linking anxiety during dating and sexual risk taking and that 'sexting among emerging adults may not be perceived to be as risky as it had been in the past'. Their study acknowledges that other than in aggravated sexting incidents, there is little association between sexting and sexual aggression, coercion, or threat, but that sexting itself may be associated with, rather than a causative factor in, increased sexual partners, the consumption of alcohol or drugs, and having an impact on identity and well-being. This is further supported by Gassó et al. (2019) who caution against a direct correlation between sexting and poor mental health. Champion and Pedersen (2015) undertook a study focused on participants aged 16–51 years old and identified that whilst the participants who identified sexual encounters on-line were more likely to engage in risky sexual practices, they were also more likely to use illegal substances during sex and engage in unprotected sex. The conflation of risk and action led to a reported positive attitude towards sexting and endorsement of subjective norms of the young people involved in their study.

It is possible then to identify a link between the motivational prompts that place the inclusion of sexting as technological assisted flirting within the context of, or to initiate sexual or romantic relationships. This finding was similarly identified by Van Ouytsel et al. (2016, p. 460) who suggest that sexting could be an indication of a sign of trust or as a gift to their romantic partner or to 'strengthen mutual feelings of trust and commitment within their romantic relationships'. This form of self-disclosure within a relationship demonstrates a willingness to make them self-known to others; and that trusting a partner with personal information plays an important part in the formation of romantic relationships. Therefore, the sharing of personal images or messages can be interpreted as playing a similar role in creating a feeling of intimacy between partners.

One increased risk that is often referenced within studies is the potential for a link between sexting practice and access to on-line pornography. Mowlabocus (2007, p. 64) noted that for men, pornography 'increasingly provides a cultural framework through which sexual identity is produced, negotiated and maintained'. Though Livingstone and Smith (2014) acknowledged that whilst it is widely accepted that adolescents may deliberately access pornographic images and films, it is unlikely they will fully disclose this fact. It is important to differentiate between access to images that are deliberately sought and accidental exposure through Internet 'pop-ups' and misleadingly named websites. Livingstone and Smith (2014) identified that when asked about intentionally seeking explicit movies or images only 9% of teenagers with the average age of 17 years said that they had not sought such material.

Stanley et al. (2018) in their pan-European study showed a discernible pattern that as teenagers got older their access to porn reduced once they were engaged in in-person sexual relationships. The hypothesis underpinning their study was that there was a correlation between accessing pornography and engaging in sexting behaviour. However, their study showed that despite England having the highest rates for sending and receiving sexually explicit messages, the reported access to pornography was the lowest in the European participant countries. This was contrasted with Cyprus who had the lowest sexting rates in their youth population, but the highest declared access to on-line pornography.

Skoog et al. (2013) challenged the concept that a boy's interest in sex, sexual activity, and access to on-line images was directly influenced by a peer-normative pressure, doing it because everyone else was, but more directly linked to the stage-normative measure of pubertal development. Their study demonstrated that boys have little insight into what other adolescents do on-line but are driven by the maturation process and the development of secondary sexual characteristics to consume explicit material for stimulation and information. Skoog et al. (2013 p. 286) found that both on-line and off-line, 'boys with more advanced pubertal maturation, on physical orientated measures, to be more curious about sexual issues and to engage in more sex-related behaviours'.

The society and culture a teenager grows up within are thought to be germane as a contextual determinant in the motivation to participate in sexting. Van Ouytsel et al. (2014) studied the impact and association between the adolescent access to pornography, music videos, and their sexting behaviours. They determined that there was a correlation between access to pornography and music videos and sexual activity off-line and a link to virtual sexual experimentation through sexting. This link between music video watching and sexting held true for the male teenagers aged 15 years to 21 years within their survey, but less so for the female participants. They postulate that music videos and pornography are more likely to portray a dominant, active sexual male role and demonstrate a submissive role for girls.

Van Oosten and Vandenbosch (2017) theorised that a teenager's engagement in 'sexy self-presentation' on social media sites would both encourage more self-exposure and stimulate others to enact similar behaviour. This hypothesis was based on the social cognitive theory that behaviour is learnt from peers; however, their research did not uphold the theory in the participating males. Whilst they reported some truth in the effect on females, they concluded that the participation for boys in sexting was driven by desire and the societal expectation they felt to act on their impulses. Benotsch et al. (2013) did find however that whilst 68.2% of teenagers reported not having sex with a new partner after sexting, those that did were more likely to have more sexual partners, participate in unprotected vaginal or anal sex, and were likely to have a higher incidence of sexually transmitted diseases. They also reported that the incidence of substance and drug use was associated with sexting.

Whilst Benotsch and his colleagues linked increased drug use to sexting, their study reported that drugs and alcohol were more often associated with post-coital situations than sexting. Their study showed that participants who were active sexters were also more likely to engage in the use of substances and initiate higher risk sexual practices than those who were passive recipients of a sext. This finding is repeated in work by Morelli et al. (2021, p. 140) who reported 'high users of sexting reported doing more sexting during substance use compared to moderate or low users of sexting'.

Gassó et al. (2019) identified that whilst much of the published research asserts a link between the impact that sexting has on poor psychological well-being and a detrimental effect on teenage mental health, there is little empirical evidence. The reason for this equivocal finding is that the majority of published studies do not differentiate between aggravated and experimental sexting. Ševcíková (2016) found that whilst there was an indication in her study that sexting was linked to psychological problems, when the results were analysed and adjusted to accommodate sociodemographic data and known mental health conditions that there was no association with depression or anxiety.

'Sexting behaviours and suicidal thoughts are risky behaviours in the adolescent population, which tend to appear in conjunction' according to Gassó et al. (2019, p. 2364). However, their study continues to argue that where depression may be linked to aggravated sexting and those teenagers who have depressive symptoms might have fewer coping skills when pressured by peers to engage in sexting. The hypothesis put forward is that sexting in early adolescence may be undertaken within a qualitatively distinct set of circumstances to those sent by an older teenager. Drawing on a developmentally contextual model, a young teenager may not have the cognitive capacity to differentiate between behaviours influenced by peers and those influenced by romantic intention in later adolescence. The impact of this would present for those psychologically vulnerable teenagers who already have difficulty coping with peer pressure, that sexting is associated with emotional well-being rather than a causal factor.

Whilst few studies associate any positive benefits to sexting practice, McConnell et al. (2017) and Morelli et al. (2021) note that for teenagers who identify within an LGBTQ+ social framework, the use of the Internet and social media sites can function as a protective factor, helping them to identify with an on-line supportive community. This then having an important relationship to well-being and the gay teenager dealing with the psychological distress associated with social stigma and discrimination.

Risk is additionally framed as having a negative consequence on the teenager's reputation and an impact on further education or employment. However, these are often the reported effects of aggravated sexting, where an image has been disseminated to other people without the consent of the victim. If sexting occurs within supportive relationships between consenting couples, then sexting, within the experimental definition, may represent a behavioural marker of normal adolescent development. Whilst sexting may be associated with risk-taking behaviours, the causal relationship between sexting and these behaviours is not as clear cut. Temple and Choi (2014) and Dolev-Cohen and Ricon (2020) note that a dominant link between teenage sexting and risk-taking behaviours is potentially subject to other variant factors. Behaviours seen in adolescence may also be linked to lack of parental supervision, associating with delinquent peers, impulsivity, and a lack of life experience. Thus, sexting is seen to be associated with risk taking behaviours, but it is not clear if sexting is the cause of, or a symptom associated with potential vulnerability.

Therefore, in terms of a substantive conclusion that there is an increase in risk-laden behaviours relating to illegal substances, alcohol misuse, mental health conditions or higher-risk sexual practices, and a boy's participation in sexting, an actual link remains unclear. Whilst the evidence points to an increase in sexual interests and related activities, that sexting is a causal link remains unproven in the published research to-date. Livingstone and Smith (2014) conclude that participating in sexually risky behaviours is increased as an association with, rather than caused by, sexting practice. They argue that the developmental tasks of adolescent appear to dovetail with the specific affordances of the Internet to develop self-identity, self-presentation, and the need to develop intimate relationships, and teenagers who are already vulnerable off-line are likely also to be vulnerable on-line.

References

Albury, K., & Byron, P. (2014). Queering sexting and sexualisation. *Media International Australia, 153*, 138–147.

Albury, K. (2017). Just because it's public doesn't mean it's any of your business: Adults' and children's sexual rights in digitally mediated spaces. *New Media & Society, 19*(5), 713–725.

Bauermeister, J., Yeagley, E., Meanley, S., & Pingel, E. (2014). Sexting among young men who have sex with men: Results from a national survey. *Journal of Adolescent Health, 54*, 606–611.

Baumgartner, S., Valkenburg, P., & Peter, J. (2010). Assessing causality in relationship between adolescents' risky sexual online behaviour and their perceptions of this behaviour. *Journal of Youth Adolescence, 39*, 1226–1239.

Benotsch, E., Snipes, D., Martin, A., & Bull, S. (2013). Sexting, substance abuse and sexual risk behaviours in young adults. *Journal of Adolescent Health, 52*, 307–313.

Cass, V. (1979). Homosexual identity formation, a theoretical model. *Journal of Homosexuality, 4*(3), 219–235.

Champion, A., & Pedersen, C. (2015). Investigating differences between sexters and non-sexters on attitudes, subjective norms, and risky sexual behaviours. *The Canadian Journal of Human Sexuality, 24*(3), 205–214.

Clarke, K., Cover, R., & Aggleton, P. (2018). Sex and ambivalence: LGBTQ youth negotiating sexual feelings, desires, and attractions. *Journal of LGBT Youth*, published online, June, 1–16.

Dolev-Cohen, M., & Ricon, T. (2020). Demystifying sexting: Adolescent sexting and its associations with parenting styles and sense of parental control in Israel. *Cyberpsychology: Journal of Psychological Research on Cyberspace, 14*(6), 1–6.

Fairbairn, W. (1994). Theoretical contributions to Object relations theory. In D. Shariff & E. Fairbairn-Birtles (Eds.), *From instinct to self; Selected papers of WRD Fairbairn, Volume 1 Clinical and theoretical papers* (pp. 200–264). E-book 2021, International Psychology Institute.

Gassó, M., Klettke, B., Agustina, J., & Montiel, I. (2019). Sexting, mental health, and victimisation among adolescents: A literature review. *International Journal of Environmental Research and Public Health, 16*, 1–14.

Gilligan, C. (1977). In a different voice: Women's conceptions of self and morality. *Harvard Educational Review, 47*, 481–517.

Hadley, J. (1989). The neurobiology of motivational systems. In J. Lichtenberg (Ed.), *Psychoanalysis and motivation*. The Analytic Press.

Hammack, L., & Manago, M. (2024). The psychology of sexual and gender diversity in the 21st century: Social technologies and stories of authenticity. *American Psychologist.* Advance online publication. https://doi.org/10.1037/amp0001366

Hasinoff, A. (2015). *Sexting Panic: Rethinking criminalization, privacy, and consent* (p. 4). University of Illinois Press.

Holt, T., Bossler, A., Malinski, R., & May, D. (2016). Identifying predictors of unwanted online sexual conversations among youth using a low self-control and routine activity framework. *Journal of Contemporary Criminal Justice, 32*(2), 108–128.

Jacobson, L., Daire, A., Abel, E., & Lambie, G. (2015). Gender expressions differences in same-sex intimate partner violence victimization, perpetration, and attitudes among LGBTQ college students. *Journal of LGBT Issues in Counselling, 9*, 199–216.

Jonsson, L., Bladh, M., Priebe, G., & Svedin, C. (2015). Online sexual behaviours among Swedish youth: Associations to background factors, behaviours, and abuse. *European Child and Adolescent Psychiatry, 24*, 1245–1260.

Kolano, M. (2013). *Subject-relating and object-relating: An intersubjective exploration of adolescent texting*. PhD Dissertation, Chicago School of Professional Psychology.

Korenis, P., & Billick, S. (2014). Forensic implications: Adolescent sexting and cyberbullying. *Psychiatry, 85*, 97–101.

Kosciw, J., Palmer, N., & Kull, R. (2015). Reflecting resiliency: Openness about sexual orientation and/or gender identity and its relationship to well-being and educational outcomes for LGBT students. *American Journal of Community Psychology, 55*, 167–178.

La Handschuh, C., Cross, A., & Smaldone, A. (2018). Is sexting associated with sexual behaviours during adolescence? A systematic literature review and meta-analysis. *Journal of Midwifery & Women's Health, 64*(1), 88–97.

Lee, M., & Crofts, T. (2015). Gender, pressure, coercion, and pleasure: Untangling motivations for sexting between young people. *British Journal of Criminology, 55*, 454–473.

Lichtenberg, J. (2013). *Psychoanalysis and motivation*. The Analytic Press.

Lindquist, A., Sendén, M., & Renström, E. (2021). What is gender, anyway: A review of the options for operationalising gender. *Psychology & Sexuality, 12*(4), 332–344.

Livingstone, S., & Smith, P. (2014). Annual research review: Harms experienced by child users of online and mobile technologies: The nature, prevalence, and management of sexual and aggressive risks in the digital age. *Journal of Child Psychology and Psychiatry, 55*(6), 635–654.

McCormack, M. (2011). Mapping the terrain of homosexually themed language. *British Journal of Sociology, 58*(5), 1664–1679.

McConnell, E., Clifford, A., Korpak, A., Phillips, G., II, & Birkett, M. (2017). Identity, victimisation, and support: Facebook experiences and mental health among LGBTQ youth. *Computer Human Behaviour, 76*, 237–244.

Mohammad, T., & Nooraini, I. (2021). Routine activity theory and juvenile delinquency: The roles of peers and family monitoring among Malaysian adolescents. *Children and Youth Services Review, 121*(C), 105795.

Morelli, M., Urbini, F., Bianchi, D., Baiocco, R., Cattelino, E., Laghi, F., Sorokowski, P., Misiak, M., Dziekan, M., Hudson, H., Marshall, A., Nguyen, T., Mark, L., Kopecky, K., Szotkowski, R., Van Demirtaş, E., Outsel, J., Voiskounsky, A., Bogacheva, N., Ioannou, M., Synott, J., Tzani-Pepelasi, K., Balakrishnan, V., Okumu, M., Small, E., Nikolova, S., Drouin, M., & Chirumbolo, A. (2021). The relationship between dark triad personality traits and sexting behaviours among adolescents and young adults across 11 countries. *International Journal of Environmental Research and Public Health*, *18*(2526), 1–25.

Mowlabocus, S. (2007). Gay men and the pornification of everyday life. In S. Paasonen, K. Nikunen, & L. Soarenmaa (Eds.), *Pornification: Sex and sexuality in media culture* (pp. 61–71). Berg.

Muss, R., Velder, E., & Porton, H. (1996). *Theories of adolescence* (6th ed.). McGraw-Hill.

Naezer, M. (2018). From risky behaviour to sexy adventures: Reconceptualising young people's online sexual activities. *Culture, Health & Sexuality*, *20*(6), 715–729.

Needham, J. (2021). Sending nudes: Intent and risk associated with 'sexting' as understood by gay adolescent boys. *Sexuality & Culture*, *5*(2), 396–416.

Ojeda, M., Del Rey, R., Ortega-Ruiz, R., & Casas, J. (2019). Sexting: A new way to explore sexuality. In F. Wright (Ed.), *Digital technology* (pp. 99–124). Nova Science.

O'Sullivan, L. (2014). Linking online sexual activities to health outcomes among teens'. *New Directions for Child and Adolescent Development*, *144*, 37–51.

Phippen, A., & Brennan, M. (2016). The new normal? *Young People, Technology & Online Behaviour*. Accessed March 3, 2023, from https://www.nota.co.uk/

Phippen, A., & Bond, E., 2023. A progressive future?. In *Policing teen sexting: Supporting children's rights while applying the law* (pp. 93–114). Springer International Publishing.

Pingle, J., Mills, K., McAteer, J., Jepson, R., Hogg, E., Anand, N., & Blakemore, S. (2017). The physiology of adolescent sexual behaviour: A systematic review. *Cogent Social Sciences*, *3*, 1–14.

Ricciardelli, R., & Adorjan, M. (2018). If a girl's photo gets sent around, that's a way bigger deal than if a guy's photo gets sent around: Gender, sexting, and the teenage years. *Journal of Gender Studies*, *28*(5), 563–577.

Rosen, N. Peralta, R., & Merrill, M. (2019). Learning how sexual minorities in school and at home: How critical pedagogy can challenge heterosexism. *Cogent Education*.

Ševcíková, A. (2016). Girl' and boys' experience with teen sexting in early and late adolescence. *Journal of Adolescence*, *51*, 156–162.

Skoog, T., Sorbring, E., Hallberg, J., & Bohlin, M. (2013). Boy's pubertal timing measured on the pubertal development scales linked to online sexual activities. *International Journal of Sexual Health, 25,* 281–290.

Setty, E. (2019a). 'Confident' and 'hot' or 'desperate' and 'cowardly'? Meanings of young men's sexting practices in youth sexting culture. *Journal of Youth Studies,* Published on-line, July, 1–17.

Setty, E. (2019b). A rights-based approach to youth sexting: Challenging risk, shame, and the denial of rights to bodily and sexual expression within youth digital sexual culture. *International Journal of Bullying Prevention,* Published on-line, November 19, 1–14.

Stanley, N., Barter, C., Wood, M., Aghtaie, N., Larkins, C., Lanau, A., & Överlien, C. (2018). Pornography, sexual coercion and abuse and sexting in young people's intimate relationships: A European study. *Journal of Interpersonal Violence, 33*(19), 2919–2944.

Steinberg, L. (2010). Commentary: A behavioural scientist looks at the science of adolescent brain development. *Brain and Cognition, 72*(1), 60–164.

Temple, J., & Choi, H. (2014). Longitudinal association between teen sexting and sexual behaviour. *Pediatrics, 134*(5), e1287–e1292.

Van Dijke, S., Van den Eynde, S., & Enzlin, P. (2025). The bright side of sexting: A scoping review on its benefits. *Computers in Human Behavior, 164,* 108499. https://doi.org/10.1016/j.chb.2024.108499

Van Oosten, J., & Vandenbosch, L. (2017). Sexy online self-presentation on social network sites and the willingness to engage in sexting: A comparison of gender and age. *Journal of Adolescence, 54,* 42–50.

Van Ouytsel, J., Ponnet, K., & Walrave, M. (2014). The associations between adolescents' consumption of pornography and music videos and their sexting behavior. *Cyberpsychology, Behavior and Social Networking, 17*(12), 772–778.

Van Ouytsel, J., Walrave, M., Ponnet, K., & Heirman, W. (2015). The association between adolescent sexting, psychosocial difficulties and risk behavior: Integrative review. *The Journal of School Nursing, 31*(1), 54–69.

Van Ouytsel, J., Van Gool, E., Walrave, M., Ponnet, K., & Peeters, E. (2016). Exploring the role of social networking sites within adolescent romantic relationships and dating experiences. *Computers in Human Behavior, 55,* 76–86.

Walrave, M., Heirman, W., & Hallam, L. (2014). Under pressure to sext? Applying the theory of planned behaviour to adolescent sexting. *Behaviour & Information Technology, 33*(1), 85–97.

Weisskirch, R., Drouin, M., & Delevi, R. (2017). Relational anxiety and sexting. *The Journal of Sex Research, 54*(6), 685–693.

Yunkaporta, T., & Shillingsworth, D. (2020). Relationally responsive standpoint. *Journal of Indigenous Research, 8*(4), 1–14.

CHAPTER 4

Research Methodology

Abstract This chapter presents the methodological design of the Sexting Behaviour study, which explores adolescent boys' motivations and behaviours related to sexting. Using a two-stage sampling strategy, the study collected quantitative data through a custom questionnaire administered via a census approach in stratified school settings. Two cohorts were surveyed: the first (2016–2018) in a single Local Authority, and the second (2020–2022) across England with added regional stratification. In total, 3987 responses were gathered, enabling analysis across age, ethnicity, religion, sexual identity, and region. To ensure representativeness and reduce bias, the study used probability-proportionate sampling and aggregated responses. Adopting a pragmatic epistemological stance, it combined positivist and interpretivist approaches to capture both general trends and individual experiences. This dual perspective acknowledges the complexity of adolescent development and the subjective nature of sexting. The study's rigorous design supports predictive validity and offers a nuanced understanding of sexting as a developmental, rather than purely behavioural, phenomenon.

Keywords Attitudes and expectations • Comparative generalisation • Criterion measurement • Ethnic groups • Faith structure

© The Author(s), under exclusive license to Springer Nature Switzerland AG 2025
J. Needham, *Addressing Sexting in Educational Spaces*, Studies in Childhood and Youth,
https://doi.org/10.1007/978-3-031-96398-8_4

As has been stated, the axiological basis for this book is to provide a voice to young people whose values are often overlooked, and to ensure that their needs and preferences are reflected within practice and policy development. One of the fundamental principles of axiology as an ethical value, in the rational feature of estimative intentionality, that every human being has intrinsic value and worth. Therefore, an approach is needed that seeks the best way to understand the different value systems inherent in each young person and the reasons behind them whilst also analysing responses within large population samples.

To identify the independent and dependant variables and to assess the underlying motivations and reasons that support boys' choices in their sexting behaviours, any data gathering tool therefore needs to adequately describe the quantitative characteristics in a consistent and reliable format. As the data collected from the participants is subjective, the tool also needs to allow the findings to be generalised and allow predictive validity, so allowing criterion measurement.

Glasgow (2005, p. 1-1) identifies that surveys can collect information from large participant groups allowing the gathering of information and attitudes that may otherwise be difficult to measure. It is acknowledged that survey completion may be subject to intentional misreporting, providing answers that a participant wants people to see or to hide what they think might be judged as inappropriate behaviour.

The Sexting Behaviour study that underpins the work within this book used a two-stage sampling plan procedure. Stage one of the study was to gather quantitative data using a specifically designed sexting behaviour questionnaire utilising a census sample strategy to gather data from a stratified and clustered target population within an identified school setting as a unit of analysis. This census data collection was divided into two cohorts both of which aggregated the individual questionnaire responses to lessen the effects of idiosyncratic or individual attitudes.

Data from the first cohort of the sexting behaviour questionnaire occurred over 2016 to 2018, with the target population being those boys who identified as male, born, or who identify as male by their choice of gender identity, in the academic Year 10 (age 14) to Year 13 (age 18) in a stratified convenience sample of schools in a large Local Authority. At this first stage, a sample of schools was drawn with probability proportionate to size from a frame stratified by school admission policy of maintained or academy school, selective and independent school.

Data from the second cohort was gathered from a similar sample of students, again in Year 10 (age 14) to Year 13 (age 18) and was drawn from a convenience sample of schools across England in 2020 to 2022. Based again on probability proportionate to size from a frame stratified by education approach being mainstream (maintained by the Local authority or an academy), selective entrance or independent provider, but this second cohort included the additional stratification by region.

The combined 3987 survey results from both cohorts, the survey was specifically designed to support analyses in relation to four key sample categories based around the variable characteristics of:

- Age range: Defined by birth age 14 years to 18 years, and by school year group Year 10 to Year 13 (or the equivalent in independent education settings).
- Ethnic groups: Taken from the five largest ethnic groups as identified by the Office for National Statistics: Asian British, Black African or Black Caribbean British, White British, Dual Heritage British, and Other Ethnic groups.
- Religion: Based on four groups: Christian faith, Islamic faith, other faith, or no belief structure (agnostic or atheist), examining the participants belief structure rather than their family belief.
- Sexual Identity: Based on five key gender identities: heterosexual, homosexual, bisexual, undecided, or those who identified within a gender diverse definition.

The second cohort of participants introduced the additional sample category, based on:

- Region: Seven additional regionally distributed identities within England, defined as Northeast, Northwest, East Midlands, Southwest, South Coast, Southeast and London Region.

These boosts provided representative samples of the relevant sub-populations as a whole, rather than drawing disproportionately from areas or schools with high numbers of particular student's groupings.

The scaling level for all variables was ordinal, with passive treatment of missing data used to ensure that a survey response with a missing value on one variable did not contribute to the solution for that variable but did contribute to the solution for all other variables, with a separate additional category fitted for missing values on each variable.

An equal weighting was given to the simple binary variables (sext and not sext). The resulting variable was subject to a normal score transformation (so that the mean was zero and SD was 1) prior to further analysis. The other data were drawn from the sexting behaviour questionnaire with further explanatory variables, organised into blocks based on the Sesar et al. (2019) motivational determinants of sexting theoretical model of the nature of various influences on sexting behaviours.

The five main blocks were composed of:

- Sexual identity
- Viewing of pornography
- Identity of sender or recipient
- Their reflection on receipt of the message
- School context: school admissions status

The division of variables between these blocks is not a rigid demarcation but is a useful way of structuring the wide range of data available through the sexting behaviour questionnaire. It was possible then to explore whether these factors influence or mediate equity effects, with the expectation to both improve the prediction of sexting practice and determine the motivation to do so.

In addition to the quantitative data collected from the sexting behaviour questionnaire, qualitative data around the explanatory variables of attitudes, expectations, and behaviours of the participants, were drawn from 20 separate face-to-face or on-line interviews each of 45 minutes duration conducted with a volunteer student. From the first stage participants, a second stage of qualitative data was sought using a semi-structured approach to interviews. The methodological strategy adopted in the use of semi-structured interviews was as an attempt to triangulate and validate the quantitative data gathered and to address the possibility in the variation of reliability, validity of quantification, comparison, and generalisation by using the words of the young people themselves. The sensitive clustering of the student background variables drawn from the Stage 1 participants were used to form a stratified selective sample based on the identified sample boosts to identify comparative generalisation and heterogeneity.

The initial research methodological approach acknowledged that adopting a solely positivist attitude to solve the 'problem' of sexting would not work as the individual circumstances of each young person requires a phenomenological interpretation to understand their situation. Therefore, taking a pragmatic approach, with an embedded degree of interpretivism into the enquiry acknowledges the importance of the 'individual constructions' when interpreting the data and findings.

School Engagement

Forty-five schools participated in a large-scale cross-sectional comparative study across four academic year groups, year 10 to year 13. Based on probability proportionate to size, from a frame stratified by educational setting provider, that being mainstream schools maintained by the Local Authority or an academy provider, and schools with selective entrance criteria or an independent provider. These schools were drawn from a convenience sample of educational establishments across England. Of the 45 schools that took part in the study, 80% were from the maintained school sector, and 20% from the independent or selective schools' sector.

The study relied upon parental engagement and assent for their son to participate. This was given by 63% of the parents or carers within the targeted academic year groups. Of this cohort 93.8% of the students consented to take part in the sexting behaviour questionnaire.

To assess the predictive value of the regression line, a measure of strength of the relationship between the two data cohorts is necessary. The correlation coefficient between the data cohorts of 0.069 and 0.066 indicates a positive correlation between the age range variables, the two cohorts covary in the same direction and indicate a linear relationship, allowing statistical significance to be inferred in the analysis produced.

Whilst the convenience sampling approach to participant school selection considered the geographical location of the school and the type of school but did not, in the first instance, consider the ethnic diversity of each school population. Similarly, the strategic decision was made that rather than the targeted identification of the participant subjects, a census methodology would be applied to gather information from all the eligible participants in each school. This approach was chosen to counter a potential population bias and address the presupposition that the different school populations represent the homogeneous views of young people.

References

Glascow, P. (2005). *Fundamentals of survey research methodology.* MITRE, Washington C3 Centre, McLean, Virginia (I - 2-5).

Sesar, K., Dodja, A., & Šimić, N. (2019). Motivational determinants of sexting: Towards a model of integrating the research. *Psihologijske Teme, 28*(3), 461–482.

CHAPTER 5

Demographic and Cultural Determinants

Abstract This chapter explores whether sexting should be considered a normative behaviour among adolescent boys by examining its initiation and progression. It distinguishes between passive sexting (receiving unsolicited explicit content) and active sexting (intentionally sharing sexualised material), finding that active sexting increases with age and correlates with pubertal development and rising testosterone levels. The data shows a consistent upward trend in active sexting, whilst regular pornography use declines with age, suggesting sexting may serve as a substitute, especially within romantic relationships.

Religiosity is a moderating factor, with higher adherence linked to lower sexting engagement due to doctrinal prohibitions. Sexual identity has limited influence, though bisexual and gender-diverse boys report higher sexting rates in relationships. Similarly boarding school students show higher sexting rates, likely due to reduced parental oversight. These findings suggest sexting is increasingly integrated into adolescent sexual development, shaped by biological, social, and cultural influences.

Keywords AI-generated images · Body image · Cultural determinants · Passive sexting · Scopophilia · Sexting content · Sexting rates · Social determinants

First Exposure to Sexting

To establish if sexting behaviour should now be classed as normative behaviour in the youth population, it is essential to identify the factors that surround the first exposure to sexting and differentiating between 'passive sexting' that being sent sexualised content without requesting it and the process of active participation in the sending explicit content.

Baker (2024) in the U-Switch survey of smartphone or mobile phone access or ownership by teenagers aged between 12 years to 15 years recorded a median percentage of ownership at 94%, rising to 98% for young adults aged 16–24 years old. With smartphone ownership penetration in the UK showing that the average age at which teenagers start to consistently own mobile phones is 11 years old, in preparation for starting at secondary school. This clearly demonstrates the integration of mobile phone technology into teenage life but also begins to draw a correlation with the incidence in sexting practice where the earlier initiation of sexting can be linked to the decreasing age of access to smartphones and devices connected to social media outlets (Del Ray et al., 2019). This data is consistent with work by Hughes-Nind and Braig (2023) who write about the incidence of access to materials on-line likely to cause harm, including pornography, by children under the age of 12 years and the need for a safeguarding intervention.

Data suggested that when examining the sexting behaviours that initiation rates have risen. When speaking to 18-year-olds their first initiation into passive sexting on average started from 13 years old and peaked at 15 years old, and active sexting rising at 13 years to plateau at 15 years old and onwards, leaving a 2-year gap between the average initiation of passive and active sexting. However, when asking the same question to a 14-year-old, the average age for the receipt of a passive sext begins to rise from 11 years old and peaks at 13 years old, and engagement in active sexting rising at 12 years old and peaking at 14 years—showing now a 1-year gap between initiation of passive and active sexting.

Sexting Rates

If, as the literature review asserts, sexting is seen as a precursor to sexual activity, then the influence of age and pubertal development and particularly the increase of sex hormones is assumed to be a contributing factor in sexting initiation rates. Pingle et al. (2017) identified that a concomitant causal link made between increasing testosterone levels, thorarche, the development of secondary sexual characteristics and physiological development was the main determinant for sexualised behaviour and the motivation to engage in sexual activity.

It is important to disaggregate active and passive sexting rates as participants cannot control who sends them explicit messages or images and just focusing on the teenage participation in active sexting rates. Therefore, the answer to the question of whether the older the adolescent boys are, the more likely they are to participate in sexting is unsurprisingly answered positively. Data presented shows that the average sexting rates clearly show a year-on-year increase, by age, in active sexting. Further this rise has continued to increase since 2016 compared with 2022 with a second-order polynomial upward trend line as a percentage increase by age giving an average rise over the six years of 4.8% in active sexting behaviour patterns (Fig. 5.1—Active sexting by age).

This was succinctly illustrated in a semi-structured interview with 'Felix' who reported that as a result of pubertal development:

Like, when you've started to become a man and you've got a topline [pubic hair] *and you've got a big willy you want to show it off.* (Felix, 16 years)

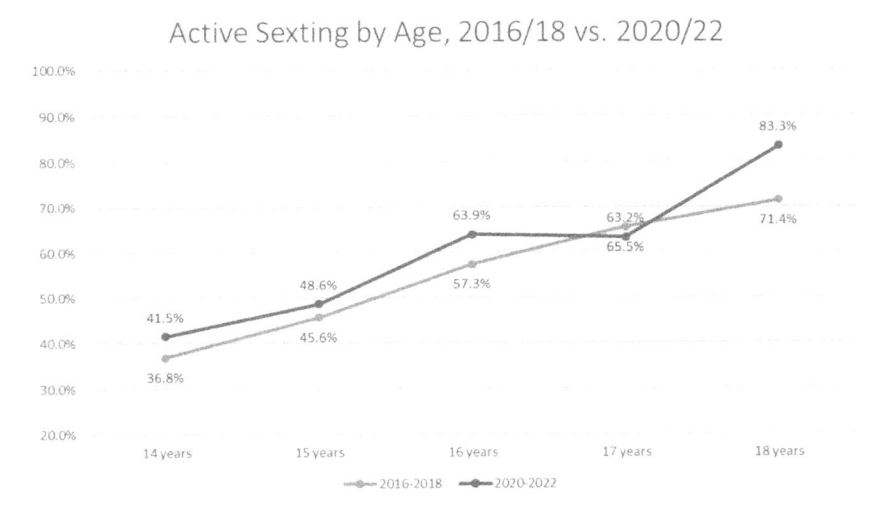

Fig. 5.1 Active sexting by age

Sexting Content

An accurate definition of sexting necessitates a complex description that reflects the wider range of behavioural traits involved with the explicit nature of any image or other message content. Reed et al. (2020) caution that a definition of sexting must identify subsets against which behaviours can be mapped. Therefore, a definition needs to consider the role of 'active' sender or 'passive' recipient, the inclusion of explicit text, images, AI generated pseudo-images, self-generated media, links to pornographic sites, and explicit line drawings.

Passive Sexting

Once given access to a mobile device, 98.3% of young men identified themselves as being in receipt of passive sexts either from a stranger or from someone they know.

When considering the content of these unrequested messages they had received from strangers, the largest percentage were messages containing images of naked women (54.3%) or topless, semi-naked females (15.8%). With filmed sexual activity or downloaded pornographic materials involving females also forming the content of the sexts. Films and messages containing images of males only occupied a combined total of 8.6% of the message content.

When analysing the content of the passive messages sent by a known sender by the recipient's sexual identity the messages were predominantly image based. Regardless of the recipient's gender identity all those who were in receipt of passive sext messages were sent images of females, explicit written material relating to females was received by those participants that identified as heterosexual, and explicit text messages relating to males were received by those participants who identified with a homosexual, bisexual, transgender, or gender diverse identity (GBT+).

Boys reported receiving images of naked women, though more by the heterosexual participants (64%), and the participants within the homosexual, bisexual, transgender, or gender diverse community received more images of a naked male (38.8%). Again, semi-naked images of women were received by both groups of participants, but topless images of men were almost exclusively received by those who identified as 'other than heterosexual'.

Active Sexting

Within the study an average of 62.7% of the boys between 14 years and 18 years identified themselves as active sexters, sending content relating to themselves. When asked to reflect on the content of their sext messages and to whom they were sent, 79.2% were willing to talk about the content of their messages. For these boys, 52.7% sent either naked pictures of themselves or reported sending explicit films of themselves masturbating, 22.7% had sent topless pictures, and 21.7% had sent explicit and sexualised messages to another person.

Of the participating boys, 19.1% reported that they actively sent content to people they did not know. Of these, 64.2% reported to have sent either naked pictures of themselves or videos of sexual activity, 22.8% had sent explicit messages, and 10.9% had sent a semi-naked picture to a relative stranger.

When analysing the content of the active sext messages sent to a known recipient, by the participants sexual identity the messages were predominantly image based, with fully naked pictures being sent in almost equal measure by boys who identified as heterosexual, or those who identified as gay, bisexual, or gender diverse. The use of explicit text messaging being used by 10% more by those participants who identified as heterosexual.

When comparing the content of the active sexts sent to an unknown individual against the recipient's heterosexual identity, the data show that as with active sexts sent to a known recipient, the sexts were in large portion, images of themselves i.e., 60.4% to known contacts, and 64.4% to unknown contacts and not text messages. Of those examples where messages were sent, these were again in a similar proportion to known recipients (25.4%) and unknown contact (22.9%).

Response to Sexting Content

In analysing the passive sexting rates, the impact on young people of these messages needs to be addressed. Published research looking at the impact of receiving a sexually explicit message as a prelude to, or part of a romantic relationship, is not clearly identified within the literature. Livingstone and Smith (2014, p. 643) note that 25% of 11–16-year-olds reported being bothered by such a message. Work by Lee and Crofts (2015, p. 464) note that 22% of recipients felt 'creeped out' by a sext. Korenis and Billick (2014, p. 99) record that 50% of boys in an American study were not bothered at all by passive sexting, however these texts do not state the research sample size from which these percentages are drawn.

Within this study this book is based upon the responses of participants who were asked how they reacted to sexting messages they received using a 5-point Likert scale from people they knew and someone that they did not really know. Analysing the data does not support the published literature exactly; for sext messages from a known person only 2.6% and 4.1% of the study respondents reported that they did not like or felt uneasy at receiving a passive message. Whilst 41.8% of the teenagers were not bothered about receiving a sext message, and 51.5% showed a tendency towards scopophilia as they stated that they enjoyed the message they had received. Showing that most of the participants either were not bothered about the passive sext or enjoyed receiving it.

However, similar analysis of messages received from an unknown person elicit a response pattern closer to the published literature, with a higher-level feeling of discomfort: with 20.9% disliking or feeling uncomfortable about receiving a message from a stranger. The data show that 57.4% of teenagers were unconcerned with receiving an explicit message from a stranger; but with a significantly lower number of teenagers, 21.7% enjoying the messaging.

Where the response to a passive sext is analysed by gender identity and message content, for both the participants that identified as heterosexual and those that identified within the Bisexual, Gay, or Gender Diverse community, the pattern of response is similar though the percentages of satisfaction with the message were quite different.

In relation to receiving passive sext messages with image content about females by those participants who identified as heterosexual, a very small percentage of the participants 'didn't like' receiving messages from a known source (1.4%) or an unknown source (7.0%). This was slightly increased where the participants 'felt uneasy' with the content from a known source (5.0%) and an unknown source (13.2%). However, the majority of respondents reported to being 'not bothered' by the content of the messages received (known = 38%, not known = 59.9%), with a slightly smaller number of the participants reporting that they were 'glad they had received the message (known = 30.1%, unknown = 13.5%), and less again saying that they 'really enjoyed' the content (known = 25.3%, unknown = 6.1%) showing a 19.2% variance between those heterosexual boys receiving passive sexting from a known and unknown source.

In analysing the response to the receipt of passive sext messages containing content about males, a more negative response was recorded by those participants who self-identify as heterosexual. When analysing the receipt of images from a known source 25% of the participants reported not liking such a message, and 15.2% from an unknown sender. In relation to feeling 'uneasy' about messages, 15% 'felt uneasy' about a message from someone they knew, and 9.7% from an unknown source. However, as with messages containing female content, a substantial proportion was 'not bothered' (40% known, 45.1% unknown). Of the participants who reported to be 'glad they received' the message, 10% reported this with regards to a known sender and 13.5% to an unknown sender. Finally, 10% of the participants reported to have 'enjoyed' receiving a message from a known sender and 16.3% from an unknown person. Therefore, receiving messages containing sexual content relating to men was not reported by the majority of participants to have adversely affected them. Within the receipt of nude, semi-nude, and explicit messages from an unknown source, there was only a 10.2% difference in the acceptance of male content to those containing female images and messages.

Sexting and the Influence of Pornography

It is important to explore the hypothesis that boys who regularly access porn are more likely to sext compared against the behaviours of their peers. In a study by Skoog et al. (2013), it was argued that whilst boys have little insight into what other adolescents do on-line, they are driven by the maturation process and the development of secondary sexual characteristics to consume explicit material for stimulation and information. This approach challenges the thinking that a boy's access to on-line images was directly influenced by a peer-normative pressure, doing it because everyone else was, but more directly linked to the stage-normative measure of physiological and psychological pubertal development. Skoog et al. (2013, p. 286) found that both on-line and off-line boys with more advanced pubertal maturation, on physical orientated measures, to be more curious about sexual issues and to engage in more sex-related behaviours and up to 25% of 14–15-year-old boys reported voluntary exposure to sexually explicit material. In analysing the sexting behaviour questionnaire for this study, the reported rate of access, by the same age group of 14–15-year boys, to pornography was reported to be significantly higher at 42.8% reporting regular access to on-line explicit material.

In attempting to understand the motivation behind sexting practice, it is important to establish why a boy may choose to access on-line explicit material other than to fulfil the biological drive described by Skoog et al. (2013). Stanley et al. (2018, p. 2921) identify that societal values and attitudes inform the research and policy decisions around the use of pornography. They argue that sexual conservatism has limited the development of sex education in schools that has meant that young people look to the Internet as a major source of information on sexual behaviours. In addition, McKie et al. (2016, p. 7) note that curriculum based within a heteronormative framework meant that young gay men sought their sexual education on-line, exposing them to unrealistic expectations and perceptions about sex and relationships.

'John' aged 15 years underlined this point in his interview:

I guess there is the factor that if yours [penis] *is relatively small there is embarrassment there. I mean people know that porn stars are recruited because they are really big, there isn't a comparison between yourself and something you see on-line, people know what average is, and you do want to see other people's.* (John, age 15)

In addition, Van Ouytsel et al. (2014, p. 776) argue that boys who are exposed to sexually promiscuous music videos that promote an active sexual role are more likely to have a permissive sexual script and sexual attitudes.

A systematic review of the influence of pornography and sexting undertaken by Raine et al. (2020, p. 6) noted that pornography may allow young people to learn sexual practices and judge their sexual performance against a published standard using pornography as a positive source of knowledge. The systematic review could not find conclusive evidence that pornography itself had a causal link to an increased likelihood of engaging in sexual intercourse or other risk-taking behaviours. However, what the review did identify was that engaging in sexual activity, including off-line flirting and sexual experimentation as an alternative to having sex in real life, was higher in those that were involved in on-line sexting compared to those who were not.

A study conducted by Stanley et al. (2018) assessed the use of pornography by a large group of 4564 young people across five European countries. Whilst this study focused on identifying a correlation between the use of pornography and sexual coercion and abuse, including sexting as an abusive practice, the study did attempt to identify rates of access to explicit material on-line, by nationality in teenagers aged 14 years to 17 years. This pan-European study argued that there is a discernible pattern that as teenagers got older their access to porn reduced once they were engaged in in-person sexual relationships. Their study showed that despite England having the highest rates for sending and receiving sexually explicit messages, the reported access to pornography by boys was the lowest rate in the European participant countries at 39%. This was contrasted with Cyprus who had the lowest sexting rates in their youth population, but the highest declared access to on-line pornography, challenging the idea that pornography in-and-of-itself leads to sexting. When the figure of 39% of English boys (14–16 years) regularly accessing pornography in the Stanley et al. (2018) report is compared to the same age group from within the data analysis for this study, a similar percentage is shown. The work by Stanley et al. (2018) however did not specify what constituted 'regular access' and had no respondents over the age of 16 years. The study underpinning this book has attempted to codify a definition of regular use of pornography by offering a scale of 1–5 with 'regular' defined as two to three times a week or more. Using this definition, 41.5% of the participants reported regular access to pornography, thus supporting the argument that English boys regularly access pornography.

In a report published by DeSousa (2023), intentional access to pornography was reported to be more common than accidental access; 47% of respondents who had seen pornography said that of the images they had seen it was mostly, or all viewed intentionally compared to 22% whose exposure to pornography was all or mostly accidental. The report identifies a gender divide in this intentional consumption of pornography. Among respondents who had seen pornography, 21% of boys had intentionally viewed pornography every day or more often in the two weeks prior to the survey compared to 7% of girls. This figure is slightly higher than the analysis of the study data shows where 19.5% of the participants reported their daily access to pornography. Comparison of the data around the access to pornography would support the interpretation that data within this study is representative of the general behaviours of English boys and can be used to describe normalised behaviour.

Therefore, to answer the hypothesis that boys who regularly access porn are more likely to sext compared against the behaviours of their peers, it is necessary to establish a baseline for the access to pornography from the population as a whole and then contrast the active sexting rates against this baseline figure. When examining the data, the boys reported that 28.9% never looked at pornography and 29.7% of participants reported only occasionally watching porn (two times a week), 22.4% declared their viewing consumption as 'often' (three to four times a week), and 11.3% regularly watched porn (five to six times a week) with 8.2% stating that they watched explicit content on-line every day. When compared to those boys who were engaged in active sexting, the rates of access and the regular use of pornography were slightly higher.

However, the rates of access to pornography increases above the benchmark scores for those who are engaged in active sexting with those who identify as heterosexual accessing slightly more pornography than their gender diverse peers, but only by small margins; 10.9% above the established benchmark for those who access pornography three to four times a week, 7.3% difference for those who accessed materials five to six times a week, and 4.5% higher in those who watched porn every day.

Comparative analysis demonstrates that there is a higher rate of active sexting in those boys who identify with a sexual identity other than heterosexual. When comparing the access to pornography by active sexting and sexual identity no clear discernible pattern difference could be established. Only 8.4% of the heterosexual, and 12.5% of the gender diverse participants self-identified as not accessing on-line explicit content compared to the 28.9% established benchmark within this study. There appears to be a commonality in the percentage data between those participants who occasionally accessed on-line material with 30.6% of the heterosexual and 27.1% of the homosexual participants compared to the 29.7% benchmark.

When examining the data around pornography use measured against age and frequency of active sexting showed an increasing second order polynomial trend line demonstrating an increase of boys limiting their access to pornography as they mature from 14 years old to 18 years old, and a corresponding decreasing trend line of those boys who regularly access on-line pornography. If this is compared to the already stated increase in active sexting by age, then the assumption can be drawn that the active sharing of nude and semi-nude images may be satiating the sexual drive and needs of teenagers rather than the use of explicit images from pornography, given the comments from the semi-structured interviews about the use of images as a masturbatory aid.

For those boys who declared that they were in a relationship during the time of the study, the reported use of pornography again demonstrates a rising second order polynomial trend for those boys who do not access pornography by age, and a reduction in regular access to pornography for those boys in a relationship. Again, the assumption drawn is that for a teenage boy the use of active sexting to share nude images within a sexual relationship replaces the access to on-line explicit images found in pornography.

Therefore, the hypothesis that boys who regularly access pornography are more likely to be involved in active sexting compared to the behaviours of their peers is only partially supported. Whilst the rates of active sexting have been demonstrated to slightly increase in the population of boys who access pornography, the use of pornography regularly decreases as the engagement in the sharing of youth produced self-generated images increases within active sexting by age. The data does however reveal that sexual identity does not have a significant impact on the use of pornography on active sexting.

Faith and Sexting

Islam places a strong emphasis on modesty and chastity in all aspects of life, including sexual behaviour (Sūrah at-Tawbah, 9:108). Islam's teaching does not view human sexuality as something that should be suppressed or repressed. Rather, as Alipour (2017) identifies, the religion encourages believers to express their sexuality in a manner that is consistent with Islamic principles and values. Islam places significant importance on the protection of privacy and the preservation of personal dignity. This is reflected within the Islamic concept of 'awrah', which refers to the parts of the body, generally from navel to knee, which should be covered in public. Within Sunni tradition this covering requires that the cloth not be too thin, and that the genitals' shape should not be discernible, and that this level of enforced modesty applies once a boy becomes ten years old (Lee & Noor, 2016). This ruling in the Hadith can then be extended to include semi-naked or nude sext messages as sexting by definition violates the Islamic expectations by exposing private and intimate details to others.

Within Islam, sexual intimacy is considered a sacred act that should be experienced within the confines of marriage, and any behaviour that is inconsistent with this principle such as looking at things that are unlawful or private body parts is viewed as immoral and harmful. The Qur'ān states:

> Tell the believing men to reduce (some) of their vision and guard their private parts. That is purer for them. Indeed, Allah is (fully) aware of what they

do. And tell the believing women to reduce (some) of their vision and guard their private parts and not expose their adornment except that which (necessarily) appears thereof and wrap a portion of their headcovers over their chests, and not expose their adornment (i.e., beauty) except to their husbands. (Sūrah An-Nur, 24:30-31)

These verses highlight the importance of protecting one's own and others' dignity and honour by avoiding lewd or indecent behaviour and emphasizes the importance of avoiding sexual behaviours that may lead to infidelity. Islam views sexual activity including sexting, by its very nature, as involving sexually explicit content exchanged between two individuals that should be reserved for marriage and any practice outside of this would therefore fall under the category of prohibited behaviour considered that is immoral and contrary to Islamic teachings.

The Qur'ān condemns the spread of indecent material. It states, 'Those who love to see indecent things spread among the believers, will have a painful punishment in this life and in the Hereafter' (Sūrah Al-Isra, 24:18). This verse prohibits Muslims from engaging in activities that promote indecency. Sexting therefore is seen as 'haram' (forbidden) in Islam, and Muslims are expected to avoid it.

In an analogous way Judaism views sexuality as a natural and healthy aspect of human life but also emphasizes the importance of sexual morality and modesty, and therefore sexting could be interpreted within the context of sexual immorality. Sexual relations are viewed as a way to build intimacy and connection between spouses, and sexual behaviour that exploits or harms others is prohibited (Ezekiel 16:25).

Jewish Talmudic teachings on modesty can also be applied to sexting. Judaism emphasizes the importance of self-control, honesty, and responsibility in relationships, and encourages the use of technology in a way that upholds these values. Within the Talmud an importance is laid on educating people about moral dangers promoting a culture of respect and responsibility. Extending the Jewish definition of sexual immorality to include sexting is complimentary to the Jewish ideal of a safer and more ethical digital world. The Torah and Talmud also emphasise the importance of modesty and the avoidance of sexual impropriety. The Talmud states that 'sexual immorality is one of the three sins for which a person must give up his life rather than transgress' (Sanhedrin 75a:2). This includes not only sexual behaviour but also sexual thoughts and desires. The Talmud also teaches that sexual modesty is a sign of wisdom and that public displays of sexuality are inappropriate and looking at 'the place of uncleanliness [genitalia] is not permitted' (Nedarim 20a:11). Therefore, Judaism would argue that individuals should consider the potential impact on their reputation and the message they are sending to others before engaging in sexting as a form of public display.

Christianity emphasizes the importance of purity and self-control when it comes to sexuality. While the Bible does not explicitly address the issue of sexting, the principles of purity and self-control can be applied to this modern phenomenon and so discourage any behaviour that would lead to sexual temptation or immorality. Therefore, sexting involves sending sexually explicit messages or images via electronic devices, is immoral and goes against the principles of purity and chastity and would be considered sinful and contrary to the apologetics of Christianity.

1 Corinthians 6:18–19, which states 'Don't be immoral in matters of sex. That is a sin against your own body a way that no other sin is'. This verse emphasizes the importance of avoiding sexual sin and treating the body as holy and sacred. Sexting, which involves sharing sexual content can be expressed as a form of sexual immorality that goes against the Christian didactic.

Another instructional verse in Ephesians 5:3–4, says: 'You are God's people, so don't let it be said that any of you are immoral, indecent, or greedy. Don't use dirty or foolish or filthy words, instead, say how thankful you are'. This verse emphasizes the importance of avoiding any form of sexual immorality, and therefore by extension sexting, as it is considered inappropriate for those who seek to live holy lives respecting one's own body and the bodies of others as Christian teaching states 'God wants you to be holy, so don't be immoral in matters of sex…Don't be a slave of your desires…God didn't choose you to be filthy but to be pure' (1 Thessalonians 4: 3–7).

Notwithstanding the difference between religious beliefs and orientations among the cultures, there seems to be uniformity in the views of all the religious sects on the appropriate sexual attitudes and behaviour. Islam, Judaism, and Christianity all prohibit sexual activity outside of marriage and so this can be interpreted to include sexting between teenagers. The Qur'ān and the Bible both stress the importance of modesty and decency. Moreover, the Abrahamic religions class the looking at bodies as an impurity and so would include sexting in its broadest definition on a digital platform as a form of sexual activity that is outside the confines of marriage and therefore prohibited. Oyetunji (2022) describes religiosity as a sociological term used to describe the effect of a chosen faith or belief system on actions and life choices, through the application of ritualistic or liturgical practices, organized belief systems and doctrines, and the desire to relate to the sacred and divine. Therefore, sexting would be considered a violation of these extrinsic and intrinsic values, as the religiosity attached to the practice and expression of faith would act as a potential mediating factor, with the predicted outcome being that higher religiosity within the adherents who practice religion would be more likely to refrain from engaging in sexting and to conduct themselves with respect and modesty.

In examining the religious practices of the general population of England, the Office for National Statistics (2022) gathers data for children, both male and female, aged 5 to 15 years and for 16 to 24 years and so direct comparison with the study data is not possible. However, within the ONS statistics 37.5% of this population group reported as Christian, and 11% identify as Muslim. They also report that 1.6% identify within a different faith structure and 48.9% stated they had no faith.

As well as establishing the family faith structure and therefore the culture a boy is raised within, it is important to note if the teenager considered themselves as an adherent to a belief structure or none to understand what impact faith might have on the motivation to participate in sexting. Pingle et al. (2017, p. 10) identify that religious faith acts as a bio-social model that can moderate physiological influences by relevant social variables. Analysis of the study data showed that for those participants who were brought up within a Muslim household or in a home where there is no faith structure, adherence to the family belief structure is relatively stable across the study age range. For those boys who identified their upbringing within a Christian ethos, there was a clear downwards linear trend with 45.7% of boys aged 14 years old following their family faith reducing to 15.7% having the same faith as their parents at the age of 18 years.

In exploring this apostatic disaffiliation from Christianity, it is important to examine the abandonment of, renunciation, or within a broader context of embracing an opinion that is contrary to their families' previous religious beliefs structure. Analysis showed a decline in boys identifying within the Church of England denomination from 45% aged 14 years to 11.1% at 18 years old. Boys who identified as being raised within a Roman Catholic heritage showed a stable adherence from 14 to 17 years, then an apostacy of 22% by the age of 18 years. Boys who identify within an evangelical or Pentecostal expression of Christianity, and to a lesser extent of boys who grow within another Christian denomination demonstrate a rise in their adherence to the family faith as they grow older.

If, as previously stated, the Abrahamic religions view sexting as a form of sexual activity that is outside the confines of marriage and therefore prohibited, it would be expected that active sexting rates will be lower in those adherents who practice these religions. This assumption is supported by work undertaken by Reed et al. (2020, p. 8) who predict that teenagers with a higher level of reported religiosity have a less permissive attitude to sexual behaviours and would be less accepting of sexting behaviours. However, analysis of the study data reveals an insignificant difference in the passive sexting rates between those who profess a faith and those who do not.

Analysing the episodes of active sexting by religious identity, it can be seen that 38.4% of the boys from the Shia Muslim sect, 21.6% of Sunni Muslim participants, and 10% of Deobandi Muslim boys giving an average of 24.4% of adherents to Islam participate in active sexting. For the boys who identified themselves as Christian, the average for participating in sexting was 55.6%, with those boys from within the Church of England or a Pentecostal background sexting at a slightly higher rate (60% and 58.8% respectively). Of those participants who self-identify as Atheist, the data shows that 66.1% have participated in active sexting, whilst of those boys who identify as Sikh or a follower of a different faith, identify as having no religion or are agnostic in their beliefs report an involvement in active sexting within a range of 50% to 52.5% (Fig. 5.2—Active sexting by faith).

Sesar et al. (2019) propose that children brought up in traditional societies that have a strong influence on sexual expression and behaviours will exhibit less permissive attitudes. This is supported by free text comments made by the participants on the sexting behaviour questionnaire:

Blocked the sender 'cos it is haram [forbidden], *against my religion.* (age 15)

As a Christian, I believe it is wrong to exploit a girl. (age 15)

D'Shawn' also raised the influence his faith has on his sexting behaviour:

Me personally, now because I'm a Christian I stopped doing that but yeah for a long time...The general overseer of my church is named [name deleted] and he wrote a book about like young people having sex, and our youth leader was preaching to us about it so definitely opened my mind to the

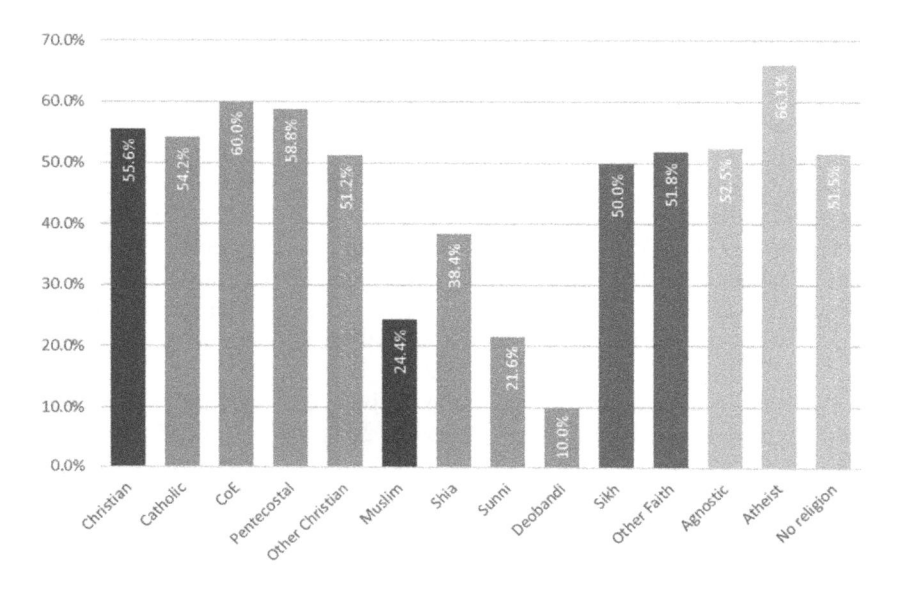

Fig. 5.2 Active sexting by faith

dangers of it and why it is bad, like kind of scaring away that like… and now I'm like 'Lord, there's no way I am doing this again'. (D'Shawn, age 17)

Therefore, when looking at those boys who do participate in active sexting it is those boys who are followers of Islam, in any of its different sects, where it would appear that adherence to faith acts as an influencing factor on a boy's sexting behaviour. However, boys who follow Christianity, another faith, or are unsure of their belief structure (i.e., declare themselves as agnostic or where areligious rationalism was the prevalent expression), adherence to a belief system does not seem to have an impact on the motivation to sext.

Relationships and Active Sexting by Faith Group

As well as establishing the family faith structure, and if they considered themselves as an adherent to a belief structure the participants identified that they were or had been in a relationship in the previous 12 months of their life. Whilst the study identified that many were in a relationship, the individual results by faith group demonstrate clear differences.

For those boys who did not identify as having a religious faith structure governing their lives, whilst participation in active sexting within a relationship was higher than the average rate for other atheists who were not in a relationship it was only by a small margin of 9.7%. For those boys who identified within a denomination of Christianity, the difference between those in a relationship but did not sext and those in a relationship who did was a difference of 38%, for those boys within the Muslim faith the difference was 52.7% and for those boys who were followers of other faiths (including Sikhism, Judaism) the increase was 30.5%.

This would indicate that holding a religious belief structure and following a faith reduces the likelihood of boys being in a relationship during their formative teenage years, but if they are in a romantic relationship the involvement in active sexting is *on par* with the expected norm.

Relationships, Sexual Identity, and Active Sexting

Rates of active sexting between known persons is similar for those boys who identify as heterosexual or homosexual, 72.3% and 78.8% respectively, with the rates of active sexting to strangers is significantly higher in boys who identify as homosexual or gender diverse, with a 15.2% difference from their heterosexual peers.

Analysing the study data by sexual identity, relationships and active sexting presents a similar picture for those participants who identified as heterosexual where there is an increase in likelihood of participating in active sexting. However, when analysing the difference between those participants who identify as homosexual, bisexual, or gender diverse (including transgender), the trend towards increased participation in active sexting is demonstrated by increasing age groups, and the higher incidence in the sharing of explicit messages whilst in a romantic relationship is clearly demonstrated.

Again, the data demonstrates that whilst being in a relationship significantly increases the likelihood of a participants involvement in sexting, the trend analysis around the sexual identity of the participant follows a similar increase with age, with the exception of those participants who identify as bisexual or gender diverse where their rates of active sexting during a relationship are higher than the average.

Sexting and Ethnicity

The receipt of sexual messages as passive sexts and the sending of active sexting with all ethnic groups are broadly similar except for those participants of Asian British Heritage and would have confirmed the hypothesis. However, there is only a 9% difference in both active sexting rates between White British and Asian Heritage teenage boys, indicating that ethnicity has a limited impact on prevalence and practice. When looking at the participation in sexting by ethnic groups, the active sexting rates between White British, Dual Heritage, Black British, and Other heritages differ with a small range of 3.4%, from 32.4% to 35.8%, and Asian British participating 9% less than their White British peers. Therefore, participants from a British Asian heritage participate in sexting significantly less than their peers from a White British, Dual Heritage, or Black British background.

'David' a 17-year-old participant noted this phenomenon:

> Back in the days you hardly see, I mean of my Asian friends you'd hardly see them with a Phone so I think now that you know that kids are getting phones at younger age and like cultures are not being a strict as they were before because societies, so that society is changing and like, they are making it like, it's like if you don't have a phone it's a bit odd, so now more people are having a phone so it's more access to a lot of things. (David, 17 years)

Ethnicity, Relationships, and Active Sexting

Choi et al. (2019) discussed the impact of ethnicity and economic status on sexting rates in the United States without drawing any significant conclusion; however, the analysis on ethnicity within this study has shown in a post-hoc non-parametric analysis of the active sexting rates that ethnicity has a significant impact when comparing sexting behaviours between different ethnic groups of boys. Therefore, 'ethnicity' appears to have a partially limiting impact on the prevalence of sexting. The receipt of sexual messages as a passive sext and the sending of active sexting with all ethnic groups are broadly similar with the exception of those participants of Asian British Heritage and would have upheld the difference in both active and passive sexting rates between White British, and Asian Heritage teenage boys indicating that ethnicity has a limiting impact on practice.

Looking then at the impact of relationships and ethnicity on the rates of active sexting, the mean percentage for active sexting within a relationship is 62.7% across all ethnic groups and the ages 14 years to 18 years. If the assumption that relationships are more common in boys who identify as White British, then the active sexting rates within that group should be higher.

School Designation, Relationships, and Active Sexting

The data demonstrates that those teenage boys in independent boarding school settings are more likely to be engaged in active sexting than their state or grammar school peers. Study participants were drawn from a frame stratified by educational setting provider, being mainstream schools governed by a Local Authority or an Academy provider, and schools with selective entrance criteria or an independent provider. The data was analysed then dividing these designations into either schools where pupils attended each day or were attending the school as a boarding pupil. As with the other analysis sub-groups the mean percentage for active sexting within a relationship is 68.1% across all designated schools and the ages 14 years to 18 years.

Analysis of data relating to active sexting, relationship status, and school designation shows that the average active sexting rates of those boys in a relationship within a day attendance school mirror the polynomial trend of the whole cohort average, with a minimal variant deviation age 14 and 15 years, then with a +4.3% positive variance at age 17 years. When looking at the data relating to boys at boarding school, it shows that whilst the average active sexting rates of those boys in a relationship within a boarding school mirror the cohort average, but that there is a much greater variant deviation of +11.8% age 14 years, then with an increasing positive gap of +8.7% positive variance at age 16 years, +13.5% positive variance at age 17 years, reducing to a variance gap of +3.1% at 18 years old.

It is demonstrated that active sexting rates are higher in a boarding school setting than a school where boys attend each day. Boys living at the school will be away from their family residence and wider community and therefore separated from friends including any established, existing romantic relationships. Reed et al. (2020) note that for those couples separated by long distance or those in isolation, sexting represents an expression of sexual contact and serve as the means to maintain a long-distance relationship. This is identified in work by Maes and Vandenbosch (2022) who identified relational anxiety in teenagers who were separated during the Covid pandemic and showed an increased need for affirmation of their partner or a person who is not (yet) their partner as within an adolescent's first romantic relationship.

Whilst there may be many explanations to this phenomenon, it can be argued the factors surrounding living in boarding school accommodation and therefore by definition are more likely to be separated from home-based relationships, combined with Capable Guardians who do not have the same degree of parental oversight as happens at home could account for the difference in the sexting practice between state and private education delivered at a boarding school. Turvey and Freeman (2014) comment on the research concept of Routine Activity Theory to define three elements that enable an activity to proceed:

- Absence of capable guardians
- Motivated offenders
- Suitable targets

Using the lens of Routine Activity Theory to explain behaviours, Mohammad and Nooraini (2021) argue that based on the theory's three main components—the absence of a capable guardian, the existence of a motivated offender, and a suitable target—delinquency-based behaviour can be explained if sexting is viewed as delinquent behaviour.

To understand and apply Routine Activity Theory to the principles of sexting, is that an action generally occurs where there is both the opportunity and ability to commit it. This is dictated by the motivation of the offender, the availability of the victim, and the lack of capable guardians. Within the dimensions of sexting and Routine Activity Theory the 'Capable Guardians' are those individuals whose presence, acting as a contextual determinant, discourages the participation in sexting activity.

In applying this theoretical application of these three criteria within a boarding school setting and then applying them to the issue of sexting, Holt et al. (2016) makes the argument, in relation to on-line sexual conversations, the school boarding system becomes the capable guardian and the absence of a 'capable guardian' is represented through the lack of an adequate parental monitoring role model either in-person in the form of persons, family members, teacher or in a boarding school setting staff, employed as house parents or pastoral support, or as monitoring software. That the teenager wanting to maintain contact with a romantic association undertakes the role of the 'motivated offender', and the recipient of the active sexting message would represent the 'suitable target'. The impact of the sexting behaviour is then determined by the sext message being either an aggravated or experimental sexting incident. In a mutually consensual experimental arrangement, the targeted 'victim' may be selected in advance specifically because of an existing romantic relationship with the sexter or be a selected partner for sexual interaction by virtue of having traits that a teenage boy views as desirable or necessary for the satisfaction of a particular fantasy. This viewpoint therefore provides a theoretical solution that would account for the higher rate of active sexting identified in the boarding school setting.

Chapter Summary

In summary then, this chapter has identified that the increased prevalence of mobile phone technology and access to the Internet into teenage life draws a clear correlation with the incidence in sexting practice, where the earlier initiation of sexting can be linked to the earlier age at which teenagers have access to smartphones and devices. Data shows that the average sexting rates clearly show a year-on-year increase, by age, in active sexting and that this rise has continued to increase since 2016 compared with 2022 with a percentage increase of an average over the six years of 4.8% in active sexting behaviour patterns.

It has been shown that an interpretation of the Abrahamic religions of Islam, Judaism, and Christianity can view sexting as a form of sexual activity and as such an activity when undertaken outside the confines of marriage would be considered prohibited.

Analysis of the study data revealed in general a difference in the active sexting rates of those with a professed faith that were only marginally lower than their atheist or areligious peers showing that boys with an active or ambivalent to faith are only slightly less likely to sext demonstrating that the practice of a faith does not serve as an inhibiting factor in sexting. There was one notable exception to this finding in those boys who are followers of Islam, in any of the different sects, where it would appear that faith acts as a clear influencing factor with an average 30% reduction in sexting behaviour.

Finally, this chapter has demonstrated that the sexting rates exhibited in boys attending a boarding school setting is higher than those boys who attend school each day but live at home. Boys living at the school are away from their family and wider community and therefore separated from friends including any established, existing romantic relationships. It is argued that whilst technology allows contact to be maintained, the reduced impact of a controlling social determinant, in the boarding environment and parental supervision facilitates an increased participation in sexting.

REFERENCES

Alipour, M. (2017). Essentialism and Islamic theology of homosexuality: A critical reflection on an essentialist epistemology toward same sex desires and acts in Islam. *Journal of Homosexuality, 64*(14), 1930–1942.

Baker, N. (2024). *UK mobile phone statistics, 2024.* Accessed January 3, 2025, from https://www.uswitch.com/mobiles/studies/mobile-statistics/#uk-mobile-phone-user-statistics

Choi, H., Van Mori, C., Ouytsel, J., Madigan, S., & Temple, J. (2019). Adolescent sexting involvement over 4 years and associations with sexual activity. *Journal of Adolescent Health, 65*, 738–744.

Del Ray, R., Ojeda, M., Cassas, J., Mora-Merchán, J., & Elipe, P. (2019). Sexting among adolescents: The emotional impact and influence of the need for popularity. *Frontiers in Psychology, 10*(1828), 1–11.

DeSousa, R. (2023). *A lot of it is actually just abuse. Young people and pornography'* Children's Commissioner.

Holt, T., Bossler, A., Malinski, R., & May, D. (2016). Identifying predictors of unwanted online sexual conversations among youth using a low self-control and routine activity framework. *Journal of Contemporary Criminal Justice, 32*(2), 108–128.

Hughes-Nind, J., & Braig, L. (2023). *Measuring online harms exposure among children* (pp. 1–39). Social Finance.

Korenis, P., & Billick, S. (2014). Forensic implications: Adolescent sexting and cyberbullying. *Psychiatry, 85*, 97–101.

Lee, M., & Crofts, T. (2015). Gender, pressure, coercion, and pleasure: Untangling motivations for sexting between young people. *British Journal of Criminology, 55*, 454–473.

Lee, N., & Noor, Z. (2016). Islam or progress of the nation: An assessment of the aurat issue in Malay newspapers and magazines in the 1930s. *Malaysian Journal of Society and Space, 12*(6), 43–50.

Livingstone, S., & Smith, P. (2014). Annual research review: Harms experienced by child users of online and mobile technologies: The nature, prevalence, and management of sexual and aggressive risks in the digital age. *Journal of Child Psychology and Psychiatry, 55*(6), 635–654.

Maes, C., & Vandenbosch, L. (2022). Physically distant, virtually close: Adolescents' sexting behaviors during a strict lockdown period of the COVID-19 pandemic. *Computers in Human Behavior, 126*, 1–12.

McKie, R., Milhausen, R., & Lachowsky, N. (2016). Hedge you bets': Technology's role in young gay men's relationship challenges. *Journal of Homosexuality*, Published on-line, April, 1–20.

Mohammad, T., & Nooraini, I. (2021). Routine activity theory and juvenile delinquency: The roles of peers and family monitoring among Malaysian adolescents. *Children and Youth Services Review, 121*(C), 105795.

Office for National Statistics. (2022). Accessed 06/02/23, from https://explore-education-statistics.service.gov.uk/data-tables/fast-track/fdf8e3d7-4420-441d-8084-6a8d82ff4bea

Oyetunji, Y (2022). *Pornography viewing predictors among secondary school adolescents in Illinois, Chicago.* Accessed Jun 21, 2023, from https://www.researchgate.net/publication/362479179_PORNOGRAPHY_VIEWING_PREDICTORS_AMONG_SECONDARY_SCHOOL_ADOLESCENTS_IN_ILLINOIS_CHICAGO

Pingle, J., Mills, K., McAteer, J., Jepson, R., Hogg, E., Anand, N., & Blakemore, S. (2017). The physiology of adolescent sexual behaviour: A systematic review. *Cogent Social Sciences, 3*, 1–14.

Raine, G., Khouja, C., Scott, R., Wright, K., & Sowden, A. (2020). Pornography use and sexting amongst children and young people: A systematic overview of reviews. *Systematic Reviews, 9*(283), 1–12.

Reed, L., Boyer, M., Meskunas, H., Tolman, R., & Ward, M. (2020). How do adolescents experience sexting in dating relationships? Motivations to sext and responses to sexting requests from dating partners. *Children and Youth Services Review, 109*(104696), 1–10.

Sesar, K., Dodja, A., & Šimić, N. (2019). Motivational determinants of sexting: Towards a model of integrating the research. *Psihologijske Teme, 28*(3), 461–482.

Skoog, T., Sorbring, E., Hallberg, J., & Bohlin, M. (2013). Boy's pubertal timing measured on the pubertal development scales linked to online sexual activities. *International Journal of Sexual Health, 25*, 281–290.

Stanley, N., Barter, C., Wood, M., Aghtaie, N., Larkins, C., Lanau, A., & Överlien, C. (2018). Pornography, sexual coercion and abuse and sexting in young people's intimate relationships: A European study. *Journal of Interpersonal Violence, 33*(19), 2919–2944.

Turvey, B., & Freeman, J. (2014). *Victim lifestyle exposure*. In B. Turvey (Ed.), *Forensic victimology* (2nd ed., pp. 143–176). Academic.

Van Ouytsel, J., Ponnet, K., & Walrave, M. (2014). The associations between adolescents' consumption of pornography and music videos and their sexting behavior. *Cyberpsychology, Behavior and Social Networking, 17*(12), 772–778.

CHAPTER 6

Determinant Cognitive and Intimate Characteristics

Abstract This chapter explores how sexual identity and sexting behaviours are shaped by cultural, historical, and social influences, drawing on the theory that sexuality is not fixed but constructed through societal discourse. Sexting, particularly among adolescents, reflects these evolving norms. Data shows that boys who engage in active sexting, especially those doing so occasionally or frequently, tend to use self-generated images and videos, often shared via social media. Being in a relationship significantly increases the likelihood of sexting, though other factors such as the number of relationships, religious beliefs, ethnicity, sexual orientation, and school type. For some, particularly within the gay community, sexting may serve as a means of identity expression and social belonging, outweighing potential legal or social risks. The findings suggest that sexting is not merely a personal act, but a socially embedded practice shaped by the need for connection, identity affirmation, and cultural expectations.

Keywords Active sexting • Affirmation • Behavioural norms • Disinhibition • Gender expression • On-line persona • Pressure to sext • Risk-taking

© The Author(s), under exclusive license to Springer Nature Switzerland AG 2025
J. Needham, *Addressing Sexting in Educational Spaces*, Studies in Childhood and Youth,
https://doi.org/10.1007/978-3-031-96398-8_6

Gender, Sexual Identity, and Sexting

In the previous chapter, it was established that regardless of gender or sexual orientation, passive sexting rates are consistently high across all age groups and so comparison of passive sexting rates by sexual orientation or identity does not add value. However, active sexting rates of those who self-identified as Heterosexual are compared to those who identified as Bisexual, Homosexual, or identified as Gender Diverse do produce results worthy of examination because of the disparity in the findings.

Michel Foucault (1926–1984) explored the concept of sexual identity and sexuality based on his theories of the historical construction of sexuality, and how society attempts to categorise and control these definitions. Foucault argued that the understanding of sexuality and sexual identity is not fixed or universal but has evolved over time and varies across different cultures and historical periods. Foucauldian theory challenges the idea that there is a single, fixed concept of 'sexuality' and instead introduces the concept of 'discursive formations' that different historical periods and cultures have constructed their own understandings of sexuality. The argument is made that society attempts to regulate these definitions and knowledge, with institutions such as medicine, education, religion, and law playing a role in defining what is considered normal or deviant in terms of sexual behaviour and identity. Instead, Foucault proposed the idea of 'the care of the self' as a form of resistance to oppressive norms and regulations, suggesting that self-examination and self-transformation challenge dominant norms and create an individual definition of sexual identity. Race (2007, p. 3) argues that a Foucauldian approach associates sexuality with the relationships between desire and power, with pleasure and subjectivity, and that this sits in opposition where sexuality is used to classify an individual as normal or pathological. The insertion of pleasure and desire into normalising regimes at the hands of therapeutic interventions, such as psychoanalysis, can then be seen as problematic.

Given such elisions, within this study, the terms gender or sexual identity do not refer to the participants sexual status at birth or sexual activity but challenges the heteronormative assumption that one determines the other, by acknowledging the right to a self-determined identity. Gender then, refers to the important facet of a self-defined identity, which can be fluid, or change over time and contexts. 'For some people, gender identity is stable throughout life and context, whereas for others it varies either from one time to another in life, or over time and context in daily life'

(Lindquist et al., 2021, p. 335). This is further explored by the development of gender expression as a social construct of sexual identity. An argument exists describing where a definition of gender continues to evolve and that as a construct 'gender expression exists on a continuum and may vary in definition from individual to individual' (Jacobson et al., 2015, p. 204). Motschenbacher (2011) challenges research with a social constructionist approach that identifies biological sex from a social gender division. The argument presented that whilst such an approach is useful to measure the naturalness of gendered practices, it does not address the poststructuralist definitions within queer linguistics around the similarity of identity, the contextual variants that impact on individuality and behavioural patterns that may not relate to a gendered pattern.

Recognising gender expression as a construct of sexual identity, this study asked young people to define their gender and sexual orientation as they interpret it within five broad categories:

- Heterosexual (straight)
- Homosexual (gay)
- Bi-sexual
- Undecided
- Gender Diverse

Jacobson and Joel (2019) develop this argument by proposing that gender can be measured against three classes of sex-gender configuration. The first class based upon a binary gender identity feelings expressed by an individual, ranging from highly binary to highly 'queer'. The second class based on non-binary satisfaction of sexual identity measured against the acceptance of a cis-like or gender diverse identity. The final classification of gender identity is based around an influencing definition of 'real', either as a 'real' man or 'real woman'. The selected five sexual identities were chosen not to diminish the self-determined expression and deny the complexities of identity in all its varied and pluralised categories that may be experienced by a participant within the study but solely to support the critical analysis. This post-structural approach recognises the concepts of sexual identity to be open, fluid, and non-fixed and challenges the notion of categorising within a binary choice of either heterosexual or homosexual but deconstructing both into the experience of the individual as 'part of an emerging cultural shift in taxonomies of sexual identity' (Clarke et al., 2018, p. 4).

The collation of statistics in the UK around sexual identity under the age of 18 years is complex. The Office for National Statistics begin their sexual identity data gathering within the Census data at the age of majority but do project a linear regression down to the age of 16 years. This would indicate that those who have responded to the sexting behaviour questionnaire can be seen to have done so honestly compared to the estimated national figures allowing the results of the study to be interpreted as statistically relevant and therefore applicable to the wider society.

Within the current study, 7.0% of the participants identified as having a sexual identity other than heterosexual whilst this is significantly lower that other comparator studies, they included data from both females as well as males. This is reflected in the analysis of the study data where the mean average age range of those who are undecided about their sexual orientation is 14 years and 7 months, rising to 15 years for those who identify as Bisexual and Gender Diverse and 15 years and 3 months for those who identify as Homosexual. This demonstrates that for the participants in this survey, the coming to a realisation of sexual identity from undecided to an acceptance occurs over an approximate eight-month period. This is reflected in the models of social cognitive development where the links between the stages of psychosocial development to the acceptance of the development of a sexual identity develop over a period of time and self-acceptance.

McConnell et al. (2017, p. 3) identify that lesbian, gay, bisexual, transgender, and questioning youth (LGBTQ+) employ identity management strategies to control their level of 'outness'. These strategies include 'who' and 'what' information is shared in person and on-line, ranging from an on-line dissociation from a queer identity to a view that content collapse positively 'allowed them to easily and efficiently come out to their entire network'. This approach was identified by 'Felix' as part of his 'coming out' story shared in his interview:

> I actually used this relationship to come to terms with being gay and actually made a Facebook status and put up that I was in a relationship with this guy, so the cat was out of the bag. I had come out to all of my friends, and this was my way of coming out publicly, but I hadn't come out to my family yet. So, I was really nervous going into school the next day, but they were all, 'OK Cool,' no one really cared, they all sort of already knew. (Felix, age 18)

Similarly, during the interview held with 'Bilal' he acknowledged it is possible to be 'out' but that the Internet and an on-line persona allow a freedom that 'real life' does not afford:

> In another way, it is a lot more private because it is on-line. You can just do it, you can express yourself as you want to be seen, rather than 'coming out.' You can send nudes to someone rather than having to declare yourself, it is easier with the internet, it is just a little bit less real. Definitely people are much less likely to show their private parts in person than they would on-line. (Bilal, age 15)

According to Kosciw et al. (2015, p. 168), gender identification is a personal matter that differs between people but for most young people does occur at around 14 or 15 years of age and that 'Identity development and particularly disclosure, is a complex process that involves risk (of victimisation)' and that this must be balanced against the increased resilience, higher self-esteem, improved academic performance, improved emotional and mental health that labelling oneself with a sexual identity that is as 'other than heterosexual' and disclosing this to others brings. This view supports current work by Rentería et al. (2023) whose research identified the benefits within an 'outness inventory' that a greater outness was associated with lower depression and sense of wellness for gay youth who lived within a supportive atmosphere but was associated with higher depression for 'questioning' youth. Therefore, a nuanced understanding of the role of outness in sexual minority youth's well-being is needed to inform school policy to address this disparity in experience.

Listening to the young people, voiced attitudes towards sexual identity are seen as becoming more relaxed. Whilst the national support groups continue to report homophobic bullying, there is evidence that a wider range of sexual identities are becoming normalised. This was reflected in a comment by 'John' who identified as bisexual, and 'Bilal' who identified as gay:

> I actually think it is more common nowadays for people to be questioning. It is becoming less taboo. I think there have always been people around, just they are more open about it now. No-one cares that much; it is just personal choice. (John, 15 years)

> I don't think it matters; a horny teenage boy is a horny teenage boy regardless of sexual identity. I think a straight boy is likely to get pictures of girls

but less likely to send an image back, where a gay couple may be freer to send images to each other. (Bilal, 15 years)

Kosciw et al. (2015) note that several factors influence this 'coming out' process including support from family, friends, and the acceptance of a gay lifestyle within a cultural, faith, or educational identity. This was illustrated by 'Edward' who described his own 'coming out' story at his school:

It wasn't easy, but this is such an accepting school, and I have a good pool of people around me. I mean I have had a little bit of hassle, but those people are a huge minority. It has been so important having people there for me, you know, we are communal *creatures, having support and people around you who just act normal around you.* (Edward, 15 years)

It is then suggested that for the boys participating in any data gathering, the risk of exposure as having a sexual identity as anything other than heterosexual may have limited overt reporting and account for the higher incidence of heterosexual status within the data.

In the National LGBT Survey 2018 (Great Britain. Government Equalities Office, 2023), it is noted that younger respondents were more likely to identify as bisexual or gender diverse compared to older respondents. Though it is noted in the report that data was adjusted to exclude responses from adolescents aged younger than 16 years. The Stonewall Report 'Rainbow Britain—2022' identifies that of those aged 16 to 24 years who identify as gay appear relatively similar across the generations in their data. The Stonewall data continues to support the National LGBT Survey 2018 (Great Britain. Government Equalities Office, 2023) that more 16–24-year-olds identified as either bi-sexual (10%) or gender diverse (4%) and suggests that being attracted to people of more than one gender is becoming more common when compared to the prevalence in older generations. Anecdotal reports from the literature would suggest that a homosexual identity would be more common, however this study's data analysis identifies a higher incidence of bisexuality, and this trend mirrors the UK Government and Stonewall reports.

'Just Like Us', a UK campaign group for Lesbian, Gay, Bi-sexual, and Transgender young people commissioned a study in 2021 looking at the experiences of school pupils aged 11 to 18 years. The data gathered by CIBYL the independent market research group for the report 'Growing up LGBT+' reported that from a study of 2934 young people aged

11–18 years that 39% identified as Lesbian, Gay, Bisexual, Transgender, including female respondents.

However, as with the Stonewall study (2022), the 'Just Like Us' study (2021), and the National LGBT survey (2018) studies are focused specifically on the LGBQT+ community, there was an acknowledged bias away from the heterosexual population, and limited focus on the students under the age of 16 years.

Whilst the sexting survey was promoted as confidential and promised anonymity unless a safeguarding issue was identified, participants were required to consent to take part. The possibility therefore exists for their name and sexual orientation to be identified, and this may have contributed to participants not completing the questions out of fear of exposure.

Sexting and Sexual Identity

When active sexting practice is analysed by sexual orientation and sending messages to someone that the participants knew 72.3% of the respondents who declared themselves as heterosexual admitted to being active sexters with a known participant, dropping to 15.9% of those who had sent a sexually explicit communication to someone that they did not know. However, for the participants who identified as homosexual; 78.8% admitted to an active role to a known person and 31.1% stated they had sexted with a person unknown to them.

Whilst the rates of active sexting between known persons is similar for those boys who identify as heterosexual or homosexual, 72.3% and 78.8% respectively, the rates of active sexting to strangers is significantly higher in boys who identify as homosexual or gender diverse, with a 15.2% difference from their heterosexual peers. However, during a particular interview with 'Alex' a 17 yr old participant who identifies as transgender, he outlined a particular dissonance between fantasy-imagination and the physical reality specifically with sending images for transgender youth:

> So, like a guy who is 15, they haven't transitioned yet so they still have the physical body of a man, but they might identify as a 'her' and then people might think they are a 'her' and everything but in the end they don't have the physical body of a woman so that like interferes with the photos and everything. So, they'd be more likely to at email, text, or voicemail rather than images if they are going to get involved in sexting. (Alex, 17 years)

This finding is borne out by previous work undertaken by Houck et al. (2014) and Dir et al. (2013) who write of the increase in sexting practice of those young people who identify as non-heterosexual being more likely to send a written sext than their heterosexual counterparts. This assumption was further examined by Rice et al. (2014) whose research identified that gay and bisexual boys were more likely to have sent an explicit message and to be sexually active. Houck et al. (2014, p. e277) developed this further by noting that teenagers who were involved in sending an explicit image co-occurs with other sexual practices including touching genitals, having 'friends with benefits', oral sex, or vaginal sex were seven times as likely to be sexually active and twice as likely to engage in unprotected intercourse than their non-sexting peers. Houck et al. (2014, p. e280) identified that their findings were consistent with same-sex sexual behaviours, but that students who sent photos were more likely to engage in sexual contact than those young people who sent text-only explicit messages to peers.

This point was illustrated in the interview with 'Alex' who clearly talked about the additional pressure and immediacy to sext within a gay relationship:

> The thing with the (gay) community is like sexting is a lot more popular like between two gay people and I think, I don't know, some people are like quite pressured into doing it. Like erm, in the way of life erm, like, a guy messages them, and they can get quite excited, and they'll be like, maybe this is someone I can actually start liking better. Then all of a sudden that person just wants to ask for nudes. (Alex, 17 years)

When looking at the frequency with which the participants engaged in active sexting, for those who reported that they had only done this once the majority engaged in sending images to both known and unknown recipients. For those who reported that they engaged occasionally or frequently in active sexting, whilst written sexualised messages remained common, the use of self-generated images and films sent on social media platforms became more prevalent.

Suler (2004) identified that users of on-line environments act in ways and say things that they would not do in a real-world environment. He identifies that this can be 'benign disinhibition' reflecting acts of charity and charitable deeds, or 'toxic disinhibition' where acts of pornography, crime, or violence occur. This disinhibition effect can be understood as 'the person shifting, while on-line, to an intrapsychic constellation that may be, in varying degrees dissociated from the in-person constellation, with inhibiting guilt, anxiety and related effects' (Suler, 2004, p. 325). This argument is extended in relation to sexting, in which the young person involved, though breaking the law by taking or circulating explicit images, dissociates from the function and consequence of their actions by route of a solipsistic, dissociative imagination, unconsciously sublimating their actions to their on-line persona to engage in sexually explicit communications with people they don't really know.

Walrave (2014) develops this disinhibiting concept further by outlining the false sense of privacy and security amongst young people using information technology. A lack of understanding relating to risk and consequence, and the lack of direct feedback and non-verbal communication, prompts teenagers to engage in actions they would not do in the 'real world'. These risks can be identified as the dissemination of an image further than intended, legal sanction and judicial proceedings, and correlates to other types of adolescent risk behaviours such as cyber-stalking and trolling. Therefore, the literature asserts that 'although individuals who sext more often might be at higher risk for negative outcomes simply due to probability, this does not mean that those who sext infrequently are not prone to risk' (Dir et al., 2013, p. 573). Work undertaken by Jonsson et al. (2015) proposed that teenagers were aware of the risks posed on-line but that young people estimate the risk they face by comparing themselves with the activities of their peers and see more benefits to an activity than risk.

Houck et al. (2014) identified a circular argument in their findings that those that sexted perceived acceptance and that this perception led to reduced inhibition that further condoned the behaviour. Van Oosten and Vandenbosch (2017, p. 43) put forward the argument that 'sexy self-presentation seems to convey the message of sexual availability, individuals who observe sexy self-presentation of peers on social networking sites may implicitly learn from their peers to be more sexually active', they argue that this behavioural willingness occurs through the perceptions of social norms.

The pressure on young gay men to present a sexualised on-line identity was noted where 'sexting-like practices appear highly normalised in the gay community' (Lee & Crofts, 2015, p. 469). The authors suggest that this cohort is amongst the most prolific producers of self-produced sexual images. McKie et al. (2016) argue that photo-sharing in the gay community is understood to be an unremarkable practice within geospatial applications; and that this is because technology affords increased accessibility to potential partners and anonymity when required, and acceptability within a given community. They also argue that the on-line world allows young gay men to explore the accommodation of their identity between their 'real self' and their 'ideal self' leading to the potential for affirmation through the sexual connections they make.

Therefore, if the perception is that the gay community is reliant on sexting-like images as a means of establishing a group identity, then to fit in, community members will produce sexual imagery. The need to belong to a community that allowed identification with peers, to engage in consensual flirtation, can be argued to outweigh the legal and adverse social implications of youth produced sexual imagery.

This was demonstrated in two interviews, the first with 'James' who identifies as homosexual:

> If you feel like an outsider, and you can't find someone who is 'the' person for you then you are going to try to find people who accept you, need you and want you – you will look for that so that you can feel wanted and accepted by society. Straight people know they can get that anywhere and so already know that they are wanted – I want to feel the same. (James, 14 years)

And the second interview with Edward, who saw the importance for him of belonging to a like-minded community:

> I think the private nature of being on-line and not having as much access to people who think the same as you, it gives you more hope, you think you are never going to meet someone who is like you. (Edward, 15 years)

Bauermeister et al. (2014), in the study of why young men aged 18 years to 24 years have sex with men, note that those who identify within sexual minorities are more likely to engage in sexting behaviour and expose themselves to higher risk sexual practice than their heterosexual counterparts. The Bauermeister study reported a high incidence of active sexting in those young men who practise insertive anal sex, a high incidence of sexual risk behaviours in reciprocated sexting but did not show a relationship between passive sexting and those who prefer receptive anal sexual intercourse.

This potential risk was amplified in many of the semi-structured interviews; 'Blake' and 'Barnaby' talked of the dangers of becoming involved with strangers, especially those met through sexting and geo-spatial apps:

> I think a big risk, particularly if you are at that age, you don't know that much about gay sex, at school they don't teach you stuff about that, it's all heteronormative so you get pretty much what you can on the internet and even then, you're not educated enough and stuff so the risks are that you could be taken advantage of, do stuff you are not ready or wanting to do. (Blake, 17 years)

> A lot of older guys in the gay community will see younger guys as a trophy, the amount of times I have gone to a bar and an older man has asked my age and then gone 'Oh Nice! (Barnaby, 18 years)

Given the reported importance images appear to have within gay culture, it is then unsurprising that Dir et al. (2013) and Hertlein et al. (2015) report the increased prevalence of sexting within gay relationships. 'Edward' described the pressure he experienced to feel accepted within the community he felt most associated with:

> The image factor in the gay community is huge, you have to meet this accepted standard, this stereotype and so if you are feeling insecure about all of this, if you don't meet up to those standards then there is a weird adverse effect, a psychological thing where you send an image to get social acceptance. (Edward, 14 years)

And 'Evelyn' discussed their perception of the role of sexting played within gay relationships within his school as a micro-representation of what they saw as the wider gay community.

> I think there is much more openness to sexting and a very much more openness to casual sex. I think people talk about the 'community,' but it is such a small group in schools that people become much closer together, and I guess that leads to more explicit content. (Evelyn, 17 years)

Whilst sexual identity remains an issue that most boys keep as a private matter or declare only with their closest friends, the views shared within the research interviews would indicate that some boys at least felt able to talk about their sexual orientation. The fact that the literature and the real-life experiences of young men who identify as 'other than heterosexual' are more likely to sext is supported when looking at the active sexting situations between known and unknown recipients.

SEXTING AND INTIMATE RELATIONSHIPS

Within the semi-structured interviews, the participants discussed how relationships develop and how sexting plays an integral part in the interaction. Both 'Bilal' and 'Daniel' described the process of getting to know a partner moving from general social interaction to an intimate relationship all navigated through their phones. The process both boys describe mirror the observations from Anderson and McCormack (2018, p. 2) who identified that a culture of masculinity can exist that facilitates 'emotional openness, increased peer tactility, softening gender codes and close friendship based on emotional disclosure' to enable a relationship. However, what the interviews also revealed was a complicated set of rules around the inclusion of sexting into a modern relationship:

> So firstly, you are just texting, not in a flirty way – then after a week it gets more, and you are chirpsing, this is all before you are going out. Then you start to see them in person, and then it gradually evolves into dating. And then exclusive and what they think is OK between them and their partner. For me, I think it starts with a person topless, then moves to dick, then full nude - a picture with a head shot implies much more trust in the person. I have only seen a headless shot. I don't think a picture of the head is the persons priority. After that it moves into films and things people do. (Bilal, 15 years)

> *Well first you are just interested in someone, but there's no name for that. Then you start flirting with them and texting – that would be 'Talking to them.' The next bit is just before you are going out with them you are 'On it,' that's when you just know where it's going to head. Well, it might involve pictures, just a few and not fully naked but in your boxers and stuff. After that you are 'going out' and then you might be kissing or holding hands and that sort of thing. It would be full photos, not pretend ones, like naked rather than in boxer shorts. But you can never ever send pictures when you're not hard, even if you are in your boxers, no one would send a picture with a flop on* [not erect]. (Daniel, 15 years)

A review of the published research reveals very little about the role of relationships within sexting. Ševčíková (2016) wrote that sexting within a relationship could be considered the new norm in behaviours. Ojeda et al. (2019) reported on sexting as a new way that sexuality is explored in young people and identified within their study that many influencing factors existed that underpinned sexting activity. These factors included self-generated images as a form of self-expression and a response to address boredom and as a means to short-circuit the path to emotional and physical intimacy. However, they reported that the primary reason for the initiation of sexting was the perception amongst young people that the sharing of explicit images formed part of romantic relationships. Stanley et al. (2018) identified that within relationships there was a corelation between the use of explicit images and an increased tolerance to sexual behaviours.

Whilst there is little longitudinal research into the impact of sexting within relationships, studies by Kosenko et al. (2017) and Choi et al. (2019) report that the more relationships a young person has the more likely it is that sexting plays an integral part within the interactions. Whilst Kosenko et al. (2017) note that assessing relationships, sexting, and the number of sexual partners is difficult to assess if a timeframe is not used to define a research period. For this reported study, participants were asked to define their sexting habits within the last year, however they were not asked to identify how many relationships they had had within that time.

To examine the hypothesis that boys in a relationship are more likely to be involved in sexting, it is necessary to examine the data to show how many boys identified that they had been in a relationship within the last 12 months. Because of the ubiquitous nature of passive sexting and the number of boys in a relationship, the receipt of a message will be unduly elevated. Instead, the comparator data examined was for those boys in a relationship and who self-identify as having sent an explicit image or message as part of an active sexting event.

Relationships and Active Sexting

Within the study, the mean of the participants identified that they were or had been in a relationship in the previous 12 months of their life was identified as 20.9%. When this was further analysed by participant age, there was shown to be a linear increase from 15.2% of 14-year-olds to 42.4% of 18-year-olds as the boys navigate the emotional growth and social interactions related to becoming boyfriends (Fig. 6.1—Active sexting by relationship status).

Fig. 6.1 Active sexting by relationship status

When analysing the study data relating to those participants who identify that they are or were in a relationship and participated in active sexting the mean percentage in the previous 12 months was identified as 68.1%. When this was further analysed by participant age there was a demonstrated percentage increase from 57.4% of 14-year-olds to 82.5%% of 17-year-olds with then a slight downturn to 76.9% of 18-year-olds.

It is clear from this data that being in a relationship significantly increases the likelihood of a participant's involvement in sexting. However, the data reveals that there are additional factors that may exert an influence on this hypothesis and including the possible number of relationships a young person may be engaged in during a set time period and the potential for involvement in active sexting within each relationship. Other factors include the participants beliefs and religious practice, their ethnicity, their sexual orientation, and the designation of the school they attend.

The gay, bisexual, and gender diverse participants predominantly sent naked images to strangers (91.7%) and reported much less the use of sexualised text messages (4.2%), potentially exposing themselves to a much higher level of risk.

Therefore, when looking at the content of active sexting messages through the lens of potential higher risk-taking behaviours, whilst heterosexual boys were as likely to send images to a known recipient as to a stranger thereby exposing themselves to risk. Those boys who identified as GBT+ sent 25.5% more naked images of themselves to unknown recipients.

Chapter Summary

This chapter specifically focused on the identification of the individual component characteristics within the Intimate Relationships and Cultural Determinants to address the study hypotheses that boys in a relationship are more likely to be involved in sexting than their single or unattached peers.

What became clear from the data was that being in a relationship significantly increased the prevalence of sexting and that boys in a relationship are more likely to be involved in active sexting by the mean percentage of 68.1%. However, there were additional social factors that exerted an influence, and these included ethnicity, faith, sexual orientation and identity, and the designation of the school the participants attend.

This next chapter will give particular focus to the voice of the participant by looking at the motivational factors that might prompt their involvement in the sending of technologically mediated sexual interactions.

References

Anderson, E., & McCormack, M. (2018). Inclusive masculinity theory: Overview, reflection & refinement. *Journal of Gender Studies, 27*(5), 547–561.

Bauermeister, J., Yeagley, E., Meanley, S., & Pingel, E. (2014). Sexting among young men who have sex with men: Results from a national survey. *Journal of Adolescent Health, 54*, 606–611.

Choi, H., Van Mori, C., Ouytsel, J., Madigan, S., & Temple, J. (2019). Adolescent sexting involvement over 4 years and associations with sexual activity. *Journal of Adolescent Health, 65*, 738–744.

Clarke, K., Cover, R., & Aggleton, P. (2018). Sex and ambivalence: LGBTQ youth negotiating sexual feelings, desires, and attractions. *Journal of LGBT Youth*, published online, June, 1–16.

Dir, A., Coskunpina, A., Steiner, J., & Cynders, M. (2013). Understanding differences in sexting behaviours across gender, relationship status and sexual identity, and the role of expectancies in sexting. *Cyberpsychology Behavior, and Social Networking, 16*(8), 568–574.

Great Britain. Government Equalities Office. (2023). *National LGBT Survey*. The Stationary Office.

Hertlein, K., Shadid, C., & Steelman, S. (2015). Exploring perceptions of acceptability of sexting in same-sex, bisexual and heterosexual relationships, and communities. *Journal of Couple & Relationship Therapy, 14*(4), 342–357.

Houck, C., Barker, D., Rizzo, C., Hancock, E., Norton, A., & Brown, L. (2014). Sexting and sexual behaviour in at-risk adolescents. *Pediatrics, 133*(2), e276–e282.

Jacobson, R., & Joel, D. (2019). Self-reported gender identity and sexuality in an on-line sample of cisgender, transgender, and gender diverse individuals: An exploratory study. *The Journal of Sex Research, 56*(2), 249–263.

Jacobson, L., Daire, A., Abel, E., & Lambie, G. (2015). Gender expressions differences in same-sex intimate partner violence victimization, perpetration, and attitudes among LGBTQ college students. *Journal of LGBT Issues in Counselling, 9*, 199–216.

Jonsson, L., Bladh, M., Priebe, G., & Svedin, C. (2015). Online sexual behaviours among Swedish youth: Associations to background factors, behaviours, and abuse. *European Child and Adolescent Psychiatry, 24*, 1245–1260.

Kosenko, K., Luurs, G., & Binder, A. (2017). Sexting and sexual behaviour, 2011-2015: A critical review and meta-analysis of growing literature. *Computer-Mediated Communication, 22*, 141–160.

Kosciw, J., Palmer, N., & Kull, R. (2015). Reflecting resiliency: Openness about sexual orientation and/or gender identity and its relationship to well-being and educational outcomes for LGBT students. *American Journal of Community Psychology, 55*, 167–178.

Lee, M., & Crofts, T. (2015). Gender, pressure, coercion, and pleasure: Untangling motivations for sexting between young people. *British Journal of Criminology, 55*, 454–473.

Lindquist, A., Sendén, M., & Renström, E. (2021). What is gender, anyway: A review of the options for operationalising gender. *Psychology & Sexuality, 12*(4), 332–344.

McKie, R., Milhausen, R., & Lachowsky, N. (2016). Hedge you bets': Technology's role in young gay men's relationship challenges. *Journal of Homosexuality*, Published on-line, April, 1–20.

McConnell, E., Clifford, A., Korpak, A., Phillips, G., II, & Birkett, M. (2017). Identity, victimisation, and support: Facebook experiences and mental health among LGBTQ youth. *Computer Human Behaviour, 76*, 237–244.

Motschenbacher, H. (2011). Taking queer linguistics further: Sociolinguistics and critical heteronormativity research. *International Journal of Social Language, 212*, 149–179.

Ojeda, M., Del Rey, R., Ortega-Ruiz, R., & Casas, J. (2019). Sexting: A new way to explore sexuality. In F. Wright (Ed.), *Digital technology* (pp. 99–124). Nova Science.

Race, K. (2007). The use of pleasure in harm reduction: Perspectives from the history of sexuality. *International Journal of Drug Policy, 715*, 1–7.

Rentería, R., Feinstein, B., Dyar, C., & Watson, R. (2023). Does outness function the same for all sexual minority youth? Testing its associations with different aspects of well-being in a sample of youth with diverse sexual identities. *Psychology Sex Orientation Gender Diversity, 10*(3), 490–497.

Rice, E., Gibbs, J., Winetrobe, H., Rhoades, H., Plant, A., Montoya, J., & Kordic, T. (2014). Sexting behavior among middle school students. *Pediatrics, 134*(1), e21–e28.

Ševcíková, A. (2016). Girl' and boys' experience with teen sexting in early and late adolescence. *Journal of Adolescence, 51*, 156–162.

Stanley, N., Barter, C., Wood, M., Aghtaie, N., Larkins, C., Lanau, A., & Överlien, C. (2018). Pornography, sexual coercion and abuse and sexting in young people's intimate relationships: A European study. *Journal of Interpersonal Violence, 33*(19), 2919–2944.

Suler, J. (2004). The online disinhibition effect. *Cyberpsychology & Behavior, 7*(3), 321–326.

Van Oosten, J., & Vandenbosch, L. (2017). Sexy online self-presentation on social network sites and the willingness to engage in sexting: A comparison of gender and age. *Journal of Adolescence, 54*, 42–50.

Walrave, M., Heirman, W., & Hallam, L. (2014). Under pressure to sext? Applying the theory of planned behaviour to adolescent sexting. *Behaviour & Information Technology, 33*(1), 85–97.

CHAPTER 7

Flirting and Social Status

Abstract This chapter explores the motivational factors behind teenage boys' participation in technologically mediated sexual interactions, particularly active sexting. It identifies four key motivations: sexual desire, perception of body image, social belonging, and aggravated sexting. Sexual motivations such as flirting, arousal, and passion accounted for the majority of sexting, while smaller groupings were linked to body image and attractiveness, sexting to gain social acceptance, and a very small proportion involved aggravated sexting with safeguarding concerns. The chapter highlights that motivations around body image are often rooted in subjective self-judgment rather than behavioural intent. Some participants expressed moral or ethical objections to sexting, often influenced by religious beliefs or negative past experiences. Understanding the underlying reasons for sexting is more effective for educators and practitioners than focusing solely on punitive responses. Addressing the "why" behind the behaviour is essential for developing meaningful interventions and supporting healthy adolescent development.

Keywords Active sexting • Attraction • Self-esteem • Curated images • Group bonding • Image content • Joke sexting • Motivation • Queer ethics • Relationship scripts

© The Author(s), under exclusive license to Springer Nature Switzerland AG 2025
J. Needham, *Addressing Sexting in Educational Spaces*, Studies in Childhood and Youth,
https://doi.org/10.1007/978-3-031-96398-8_7

In the previous chapters of this book, it has been established that the intersecting factors within key individual and contextual determinants and the demographic, cultural and social values have an impact on sexting behaviours. This chapter will look at the motivational factors that might prompt the involvement of teenage boys to participate in technologically mediated sexual interactions.

Using the data drawn from 13 psychometric options included in the sexting behaviour questionnaire, this chapter will attempt to understand the reasons given for sexting and synthesise the quantitative data from the questionnaire with the qualitative data drawn from the semi-structured interviews and the free text option given to the participants.

The Motivation to Sext

Analysis of the sexting behaviour questionnaire has been undertaken by examining the results within four main motivational categories. Bianchi et al. (2016) and Reed et al. (2020) identified three primary motivational categories within sexting: sexual expression, body image reinforcement, and exploitation. Ojeda et al. (2019) identified an additional factor focusing on the role sexting plays in establishing social status. It is important to note that these four main categories are not wholly distinct but intersect in often complex ways.

When examining the boys' reasons for participating in active sexting against these four motivational categories, it is acknowledged that particularly the questions around perceived attractiveness and appropriateness of body image are less behavioural motivations and more about a subjective judgement of self. However, this desire for boys to measure themselves against a perceived standard is considered within this analysis as a motivation for engaging in the sending of explicit images.

The predominant factor for participating in sexting (76.1%) was to further a sexual purpose within the main motivational factor with entries against a defined sub-category determinants. The second most common factor related to a perception of body image (29.1%) with multiple entries identified against the defined sub-category reasons. The third reason for sexting was where social status was considered a motivating factor, a smaller number of boys (8.4%) recognised this factor within their behaviours. Finally, the least reported motivation related to the aggravated factors that led to the desire to harm, with 11 entries within the agreed sub-reasons (Fig. 7.1—Reason for sexting by motivational category).

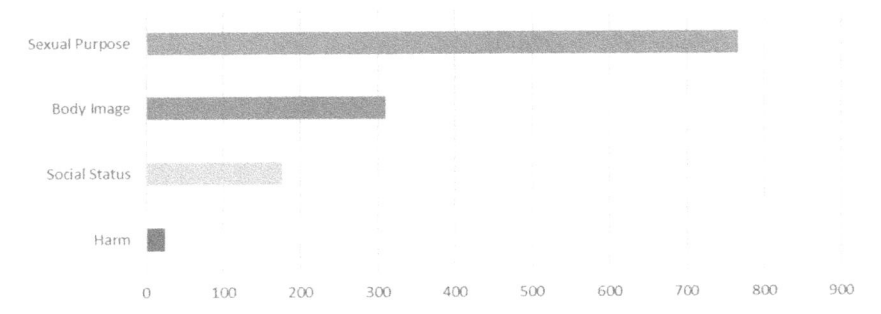

Fig. 7.1 Reason for sexting by motivational category

SEXUAL EXPRESSION AS A MOTIVATION

Analysis of the study data shows sexting is a motivational tool that aids masturbation or is part of a script within the stages of a developing or established relationship. Reed et al. (2020, p. 2) note that 'sexting may play a positive role by increasing intimacy and sexual exploration in a relationship'. Sexting was reported as an antecedent to intercourse or a new romantic relationship, with the use of sexting as a means of validating a romantic bond, by showing commitment to the relationship and to the partner, especially for those couples separated by long distance, or those in isolation. Sexting represents an evanescent expression of sexual contact or can be seen as a safer alternative to sex and serve as a substitute on grounds of faith, belief, or abstinence.

Reed et al. (2020, p. 2) note that 'although most adolescent sexting occurs between dating partners, limited research has focused on sexting within romantic relationships'. This has prompted the need to identify the key motivational factors within the stages of a relationship, with sexting as antecedental to intercourse or a new romance relationship. Weisskirch et al. (2017) and Foody et al. (2021) write that sexting is seen as part of a relationship script as a means of validating a romantic relationship by showing commitment to the relationship and to the partner. They write that sending intimate images or text shows that teenagers within a relationship feel comfortable with each other and place a degree of trust in the other person. Casas et al. (2019) identify that, particularly in boys, sexting was seen as a normal form of sexual expression and further supports the hypothesis that those within a relationship are more likely to be involved in sexting.

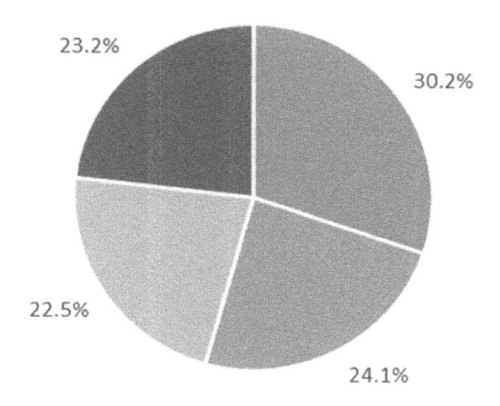

[Pie chart: Sexual Purpose 23.2%, Flirting 30.2%, Increase Intimacy 22.5%, Sexually Aroused 24.1%, Increase Passion]

Fig. 7.2 Motivational category: sexual purpose

Participation in sexting as a motivational factor for sexual purposes was further divided into four subset choices which were available to the participants: flirting, sexual arousal, to increase passion, and to increase intimacy. Participants were able to select as many of these sub-category factors as they felt appropriate (Fig. 7.2—Motivational category: sexual purpose).

The data shows that whilst sexting was used the most to initiate contact with a partner as a form of flirting, active sexting was consistently used to increase either the boy's own intimacy, passion, and arousal when contacting another person or as part of a sexual contact.

This was identified by 'D'Shaun' in his semi-structured interview:

> We see it like, if you're getting close to a girl and like, you're talking to them, you know in a sexual way, when you're getting sexual business from them like, that means that they're going to eventually be your girlfriend that, like, it gives you like, ratings from your friends because they see you 'patterned it' which means that you got her to do that, you understand what I am saying, like, ah yeah, like you sexted that person. (D'Shaun, age 17 years)

When analysing the study data relating to those participants who identify that they are or were in a relationship and participated in active sexting the mean percentage in the previous 12 months was identified as 68.1%. When this was further analysed by participant age there was a demonstrated second-order polynomial upward trend line as the percentages increase with age. When this is cross referenced with the participants' motivational determinant of sexting for sexual purpose, it is clear that whilst this forms an important element within a relationship each motivational subset was identified as in-line with the relationship average per age, with the exception of an anomalous result for 15-year-olds, looking to increase intimacy within a relationship.

Flirting

The desire to increase intimacy would indicate that within each motivational sub-category, but particularly with flirting, this occurs as a means to engage with a sexual partner before a relationship commences. This concept is proven by the analysis of this sub-category by each age group. This shows that a significant number of boys chose this factor as a motivator, with the incidence outside of a relationship reducing by 10% as the boys get older but still occurring within a range between 41.1% for 15-year-olds to 31.3% in 17-year-olds. This would support the argument that sexting as part of a sexual script now forms a key component in the sexual expression of teenage boys.

The importance of sexting as the stimulus to sexual contact through flirting was supported by the free text comments added by the study participants. These ranged from boredom, as a desire for sexual activity, and as an integral part of a relationship:

> I get bored and want to spice life up a bit. (age 16)
> Back and forth before a hook up. (age 17)
> Because you like them when you are feeling horny. (age 18)
> My girlfriend loves seeing me, it makes me feel happy. (age 15)
> To please my girlfriend when I am not with her. (age 14)

Sexual Arousal

This trend can also be demonstrated in the sub-category of sexual arousal. There is a diminishing downward trend in the use of explicit messages and images in sexting for sexual arousal purposes. As the rate of people in a relationship rises by age group, so the use of active sexting within a relationship increases, ranging from 56.9% of boys in a relationship at 14 years old using sexting to gain some form of self-sexual arousal to 75% of

18-year-olds reporting that active sexting formed part of their relationships.

This was demonstrated in the interview with 'Isaac' a 15-year-old boy, who identified as heterosexual, but not in a relationship:

> *Looking at porn is like, so you look up porn, and then no one really knows that you're looking at porn just kind of like you can 'get on with that'* [clarified with Isaac: to masturbate], *but they can get the picture from someone, you know, it's kind of more exciting, because you kind of feel that you've, they've, got something, like to hold onto, kind of.* (Isaac, 15 years)

This point was additionally identified in the free text responses within the sexting behaviour questionnaire where self-arousal or arousal within a relationship were given as examples:

Just when I am feeling horny. (age 18)
I do it when I need a wank. (age 17)
Normal and part of intimacy - just like sex is. (age 16)
Got a lot of time and I need to do things like sex. (age 15)
Both of us were horny, so we did it. (age 14)

Passion and Intimacy

The two final sub-categories that participants could select related more directly to those boys within a relationship but could also apply to those boys involved in a purely sexual rather than romantic relationship where sex plays the only part of their connection. Over 75% of the participants who selected this motivational sub-set identified as being in a relationship rising to 90% of those aged 18 years.

A similar picture emerges in the answers given relating to the desire to increase intimacy within a relationship. The majority of participants who chose this sub-set identified as doing so because they were in a relationship, with an increase from 77.9% of participants aged 14 years to 90.5% for 18-year-olds of those who use active sexting within a relationship as a stimulus for intimacy.

There being a corresponding smaller group who identified active sexting as a means to develop intimacy with a sexual partner that they considered as a sexual encounter or within a pre-relationship state.

'Steve' summed the role that sexting plays within a relationship for him:

When it is in a relationship, anyways the person feels attracted to that person and they want that person to only like them, so because of that they send nude images, so that person can only look at them or think in that way. The person trusts you enough to be able to send an exposed image knowing that you won't leak it to other people. (Steve, age 16)

Similar views were expressed about the desire to increase passion and intimacy within the free text comments made within the questionnaire. The participant comments support the argument that the participation in sexting can be used to positively affect a relationship or sexual liaison between young people:

My partner wanted to see them, and I want to be closer to her. (age 18)
I am in a relationship, and I love him. (age 17)
To help illicit [sic] sex from my girlfriend. (age 16)
To feel like someone can be comfortable sending it to me. (age 15)
In a long relationship trust is there. (age 14)

Body Image Reinforcement

Within this motivational category three subset choices were available to the participants: queries about body image and development, sexts establishing general attractiveness, and sext messages trying to establish sexual attractiveness. Bianchi et al. (2016) argue that sexting can be seen as an expression of a developmental task of adolescence relating to the definition and acceptance of the physical development that occurs during puberty. They argue that the physical changes in body appearance that occur during the development of secondary sexual characteristics can explain 'the need for social confirmation about body adequacy during adolescence and young adulthood' (Bianchi et al., 2016, p. 13) as a means of exploring their forming identities. Bianchi et al. (2017) write that body self-esteem can be seen as a multidimensional construct, one element of which relates to other people's evaluation of one's appearance. Whilst Sagrera et al. (2022) demonstrate a positive correlation between increasing social media platform usage and the development of 'Body Image Issue' thoughts and habits and the diversity of mediums and content seem to broadly have negative impacts on body image with a predicted greater impact on females, these body image issues affected the self-esteem of 18% of teenage boys within their study because of the mass-media modelling of the male physique affecting the boys perception about their own body shape and development.

Reed et al. (2020) identified seeking peer feedback about the adequacy of their body as a motivational factor for sending naked images between boys. This was reinforced by Needham (2021) whose study identified reports of sexting to show muscular definition or as a means of boasting between peers. Albury (2017) identified that some images posted by boys were an attempt to show muscle definition and could be posted on social media sites as an attempt to gain validation through 'likes' by observers. Burén and Lunde (2018) write of the impact of sexting on the perception of self on body image where sexting can be used to achieve acceptance of body adequacy from like-minded peers or act with the potential to reenforce body dissatisfaction. Sexting between peers can also act as a tool by which adolescents explore and express masculinity and sexuality and as a measure of moderation and integration within their friendship groups.

Ojeda et al. (2019) undertook a study looking at sexting as a new way to explore sexuality within adolescent development and note the importance attached to personal image and the desire to compare physical development with peers. Bianchi et al. (2019) note within their study that the trend for body image reinforcement decreases from early adolescence to young adulthood as the need to define 'normal' pubertal development in relation to their peers decreases. This is confirmed in the analysis of the study data where the percentage of body image sub-category selection in the 14- and 15-year participants mirrors the 'quadratic age-related trend, increasing from early adolescence to early young adulthood and decreasing from early adulthood to late young adulthood' (Bianchi et al., 2019 p. 7). This overall decrease in body image queries from the early teenage participants to the older contributors can clearly be seen with a peak at age 15 years of 38.4% decreasing to 4.6% at age 18 years.

When considering the recipient of the sexts relating to the perception of body image, the data reveals that whilst the percentage of messages chosen to address the concept of body image reduces with age the larger portion of the messages were directed at an unknown recipient rather than a person the sender knew (Fig. 7.3—Motivation: body image and recipient status.

Then in examining the content of the message, this sub-category relates to the physical changes in body appearance that occur during the development of secondary sexual characteristics it should be assumed that the content of the images shared would relate to the naked male form. The

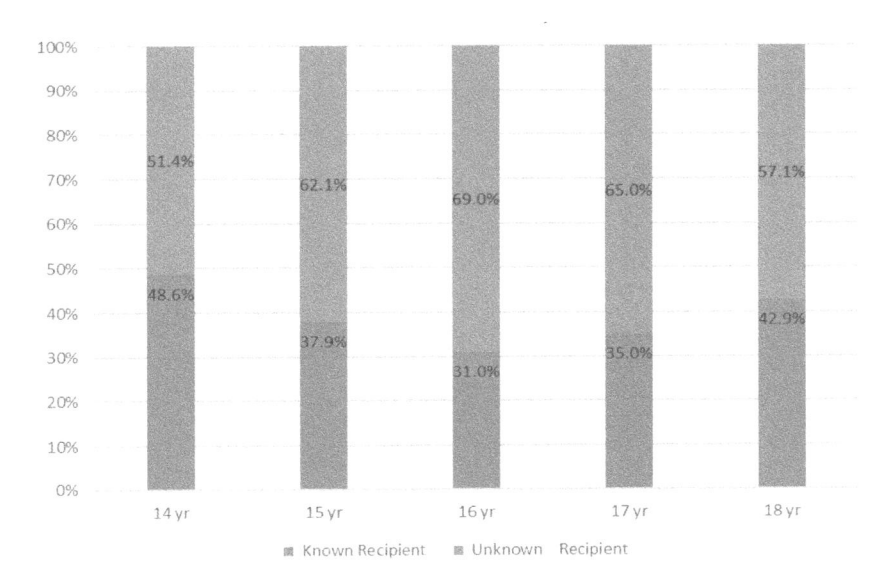

Fig. 7.3 Motivation: Body image and recipient status

data confirms this and shows that of the messages sent relating to the motivating factor around confirmation of body image 62.4% were of the naked participant (Fig. 7.4—Image content).

This finding is underpinned by the free text comments written by the participants. Those made by the younger participants relate to either penile aesthetic or a development in musculature. For the older teenagers, the comments focused on their physical attraction or the impact on emotional well-being.

> Because I am alone, sexting makes me feel wanted. (age 16)
> To make sure the other person is still attracted to me. (age 15)
> I wanted to know if my penis was big or small. (age 14)
> When I am boasting about my penile size. (age 14)
> To show progression I made from weak to strong. (age 14)

This was reinforced by 'James' during his interview where he reflected on the difficulties he had experienced as a bisexual 14-year-old compared to his heterosexual peers:

104   J. NEEDHAM

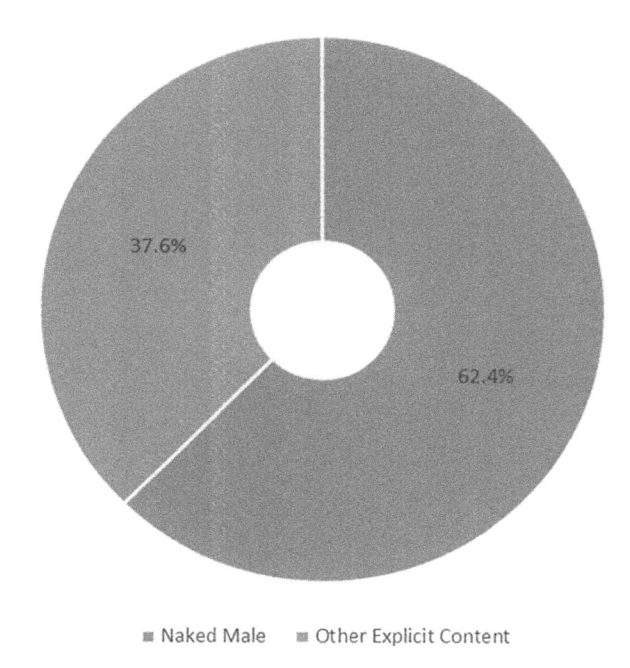

```
         37.6%
                      62.4%

    ■ Naked Male    ■ Other Explicit Content
```

Fig. 7.4 Image content

> Erm, maybe it's because it is attitude. You think differently when you are with people you like 'cos the people who I know who are gay and bi worry a lot more about their body and what they look like. I think straight boys have more confidence about how they look because they have a lot of people to tell them. Whereas if you don't have people to go to then you must find out other ways. (James, age 14)

Raine et al. (2020) report that the negative consequences of sexts being made public may affect boys less than girls, they also report positive aspects to sexting, particularly in relation to young people's personal relationships. This study by Raine et al. (2020) recognised that a potential limitation of studies looking for causal links between the perception of body image gathered by watching pornography and sexting occurs when studies do not distinguish between the different contexts in which sexting may occur. Sexting-related outcomes could be influenced by several different contextual factors including the relationship status of the individuals involved and their motives for sexting.

Van Ouytsel et al. (2014) discuss the impact and association between the adolescent access to pornography and sexting behaviours, determining a correlation between access to pornography, music videos, and off-line sexual activity and a link to on-line sexual experimentation through sexting. This link between pornography and sexting held true for the male teenagers aged 15 years to 21 years within their survey responses and identified that teenagers may be getting their education regarding sexual development and sexual activity from pornography rather than their parents or through relationships and sex education curriculum materials from within schools but acknowledge that the reported associations between sexting and behaviour may not hold true after controlling the context in which sexting occurred.

Stanley et al. (2018, p. 2921) identify that societal values around the acceptability and use of pornography and the attitudes towards the adolescent as a sexual body have a direct influence on research and policy decisions around the delivery of sex education. They argue that young people now look to the Internet as a source of alternative sex education. An argument is made and supported by Bianchi et al. (2016) that the pressure on teenagers coming to terms with body image is increased when they seek to compare themselves with images portrayed within the media and pornography and is predicted 'by the internalization of cultural and media models of idealised bodies'. The work undertaken by Bianchi et al. (2016, p. 166) argues that sexting amongst teenagers serves as a means to achieve 'positive feedback from peers and potential partners working as a confirmation of body adequacy'.

Reed et al. (2020, p. 3) caution that learning about sex through on-line media can be considered self-sexualisation and lead to a situation where 'individuals value themselves mainly for their sexual appeal to the exclusion of other characteristics where they define attractiveness as sexiness' and McKie et al. (2016, p. 7) note that learning based within a heteronormative framework will mean that young gay men who seek their sexual education on-line, will be exposed to unrealistic expectations and perceptions about sex and relationships through pornography on social media platforms and Apps focused solely on sexual activity.

The incidence of body image reinforcement as a motivating factor decreases from early adolescence to young adulthood, as the need to define 'normal' pubertal development is seen in the motivation sub-categories that challenge the perception of general attractiveness and sexual attractiveness. This pattern shows an increase between the participants aged 14 years and 15 years old, peaking between 34.8% (body image) to 42.4% (general attractiveness). This then decreases year on year until at 18 years where a very small proportion of participants identified body adequacy as a motivational factor; 4.6% (body image) to 2.9% (sexual attractiveness), for general attractiveness and for sexual attractiveness.

In each of the motivational sub-categories surrounding image reinforcement; body image, assessing general and sexual attractiveness, it can be seen that in each instance the majority of sexts was sought from recipients that the boys did not know rather than from a person they knew. Morelli et al. (2021) identified in a review of personality traits and sexting behaviours that sexting to strangers was a common occurrence. They identify that in Italy and in the UK that sexting to strangers was reported at 33%. With the data within this study (33.3%) demonstrating statistical parity with the published research.

Social Status

The importance of investigating teenage sexting in conjunction with different aspects of adolescent social development, including social competence and friendship quality, has been investigated by Foody et al. (2023) showing that whilst sending sexts and social behaviours are related to distinct motivations, they may also share underlining aspects to strengthen relational bonds between groups. The exploration of emerging masculine identity and social status through sexting is one motivation revealed by the present study. The notion of sexting as a means to maintain the masculine hegemony is explored by García-Gómez (2019, p. 316) and has been used to establish an identity based on characteristics thought to be 'normal' amongst the social group in question, but also to define how a teenage boy wishes to be seen by significant others.

This construction of, and exploration of, identity is also reflected in work by Bianchi et al. (2019), who write of a teenager's need to conform to perceived behavioural norms in their peer group. Ojeda et al. (2019, p. 108) note that 'by taking part in sexting, boys boost their social prestige and gain popularity in their peer group'. This was also illustrated by Del Ray et al. (2019), who write that the teenage boy will engage several strategies to find popularity, and this need for popularity correlates with the involvement in sexting practice: 'adolescents who feel a stronger need to be popular are more likely to post photos of themselves, thinking that posting their own sexual photos represents a strategic means for them to gain in acceptance amongst their peers' (Del Ray et al., 2019, p. 3). The perception of popular peer prototypes sexting behaviour contributes to the acceptance of the peer norm status of adolescent sexting behaviour.

Albury (2015) identified a typology containing two main reasons that young people particularly utilised around explicit photographs of themselves. The first she identified as 'Private Selfies' taken by the young person to track physical changes either due to pubertal development, or as a record of musculature or just for the satisfaction of having a photograph. The young people within Albury's study identified that these images were not designed for wider circulation, not even amongst close friends. Within Albury's work these 'Private Selfies' were framed as 'ordinary' and non-sexual. The second category of image she determined as 'Public Selfies', specifically taken to post on social media sites, or to share with the intention of garnering 'Likes'. The intention behind a 'Public Selfie' is to communicate to a peer group a location and interests. Albury (2015, p. 1735) writes that the 'boys taking pictures of muscles might count as sexting' as 'any suggestive photograph might count as sexting', and the purpose of circulating such images was to identify with a group with similar interests and hobbies.

Ojeda et al. (2019, p. 108) note that the 'desire for popularity seems to be a predictor of involvement in sexting', in seeking acceptance and increased social prestige and gain popularity in their peer group through sexually permissive behaviours. Maheux et al. (2020) argue against the notion that popular adolescents are more likely to engage in sexting activity but that they are more likely to boast about their actual sexual activity than their less popular peers but state that the evidence is unclear if adolescents whose peer-perceived popularity is 'high' will report higher rates of sexting. However, 'Adolescents were over ten times more likely to sext if they believed their popular peers had done so' (Maheux et al., 2020 p. 64). This perception of popular peer prototypes sexting behaviour, it is argued, contributes to the acceptance of the peer norm status of adolescent sexting behaviour.

In describing the development of a contemporary urban gay culture, Mowlabocus (2007, p. 66) writes that male sexuality increasingly provides a cultural framework by which identity is produced, negotiated, and maintained. His work proposes that the on-line profile generated by a person has become the most generic form of self-representation, and one by which people are empowered to identify with other members of 'minority groups who have historically been characterised as invisible'. Van Oosten and Vandenbosch (2017) write that sexy self-presentation on social networking sites may encourage similar behaviour in peers, to develop confluent attitudes, beliefs, and behaviours. Therefore, peer group pressure and the desire to belong to a social group are likely to influence normative behaviour to the point that non-participation in sexting may jeopardise group membership. This identification with a like-minded gay community can be seen to promote self-esteem and a sense of belonging to a group that otherwise feel marginalised by a comparison against a traditional view of masculinity and is mitigated by the sense of community and cohesion of belonging to a defined group. 'Queer community ethics, then, rely on a sense of sexual camaraderie and generosity that acknowledges a shared capacity to experience both public and private sexual indignities and embarrassments' (Albury, 2017, p. 720).

Paasonen et al. (2019, p. 5) define a sociocultural context where the 'curated dick pic', a naked picture, is shared between hetero and homosexual participants with other males as a potential for community and kinship without attaching any meaning of sexual identity or purpose; that the 'penis in particular, remained the key focus of attention and curatorial effort'. This was noted by Van Ouytsel and Dhoest (2021), especially in young men who identified as gay or non-binary, who describe the sharing of naked images as a way of gaining acceptance into a community.

This is illustrated with the free text comments taken from the Sexting Behaviour Questionnaire where participants identify the sense of trust within a peer group and the perception of respect and social status engendered by sexting activity:

I will share with friends who I trust and will be there for me. (age 16)
I wanted to be respected in his group. (age 14)

Clancy et al. (2021) Identify that images shared within a social group may be done so as part of a group bonding experience, and that whilst the images can be interpreted as sexual, the intention by the boys was to be amusing and meant to be relatively harmless. Of the motivation subcategory selected by the participants, 3.2% selected sexting as a humorous activity, and that this occurs predominantly in the younger participants (Fig. 7.5—Motivation: as a joke by age).

This is reflected in the free text comments taken from the study questionnaire, where the boys identify the humour and bonding experience sending images to each other creates:

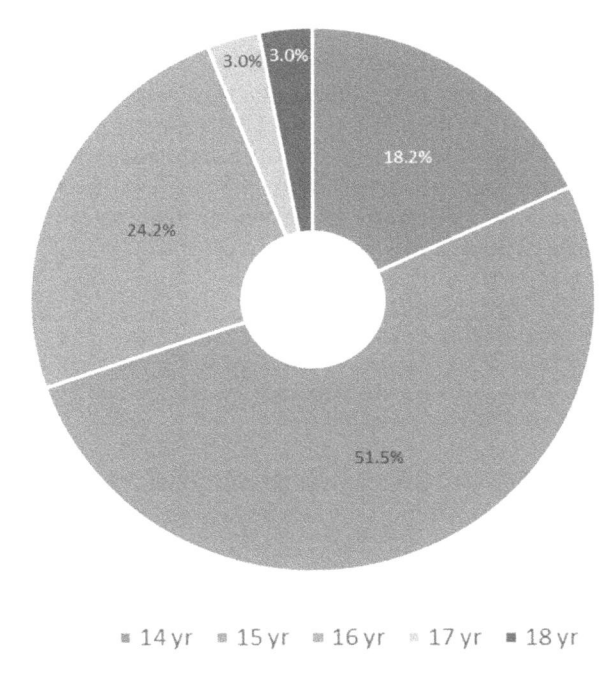

[Pie chart showing percentages: 51.5%, 24.2%, 18.2%, 3.0%, 3.0%]

■ 14 yr ■ 15 yr ■ 16 yr ■ 17 yr ■ 18 yr

Fig. 7.5 Motivation: As a joke by age

> It's just a bit of banter with mates. (age 18)
> Sent to mates as a joke, we all do it. (age 17)
> It's funny when you send it to your boys, you are part of a group. (age 15)

This is also illustrated in the interview with 'Isaac' who discussed the images he sent around his body building activities:

> With a fitness account that I run I posed topless pictures to show my like, effort with fitness and only three of my mates are on there so I could try and keep this private to the people I trust the most, but I will never like send a fully naked picture 'cause I'm not like, I'm not gay I just would feel uncomfortable. (Isaac, age 15)

One of the motivational sub-categories that participants could chose was to participate in active sexting because they needed to feel wanted by another person. Bianchi et al. (2016) identify that sexting can be seen as a key component of the teenage expression of sexuality. Therefore, the need to feel wanted within a sexual encounter correlates with the need for attachment and affiliation as dyadic satisfaction within on-line as well as off-line relationships. Within the study, 12.4% of the participants chose this motivational factor. Underpinning the comments written were three themes. The first reason was to establish that with in their existing relationship their partner's desire for them was present, the second, to give pleasure to their partner, and finally to gain pleasure:

> For the pleasure of my partner. (age 17)
> To make sure the other person is still attracted to me. (age 15)
> My girlfriend loves seeing me, and it makes me feel happy. (age 15)
> Made me feel good about myself. (age 15)
> To see if she would like me more. (age 14)

Of the participants who selected the motivational point 'to feel wanted' the majority were from within the younger year groups reducing in those aged 17 years and 18 years old (Fig. 7.6—Motivation: to feel wanted).

García-Gómez (2019) notes that whilst the practice of exchanging images may not demonstrate a motivation to intentionally harm the other person, it may be a demonstration of one partner putting their needs ahead of the other, rather than a deliberate subjugation of the other. Therefore, the demarcation between sexting as a normal act within the developing adolescent sexual agency and with intent to harm is one that is both blurred and easily crossed. The intent to obtain or share images and sexual information to intentionally intimidate or harm another with malicious intent, must be viewed as forms of sexual harassment and sexual violence.

Within the Sexting Behaviour Questionnaire, the motivational factor 'In Exchange for a Favour' was initially included as an indicator of aggravated sexting—where an image or message was used as currency between offending peers, or to objectify the participant. Within the study 3.1% participants selected this sub-category item. Each participant was spoken to before the end of the data collection session to establish the detail behind their chosen selection. In each case, the reason was given was a reciprocal arrangement with a known person to elicit either images in return, to initiate sexual activity, or to maintain sexual passion within a long-distance relationship:

> To keep sexual passion over long distance. (age 17)
> To have sex with my girlfriend. (age 16)
> To get nudes back. (age 14)

■ 14 yr ■ 15 yr ■ 16 yr ■ 17 yr ■ 18 yr

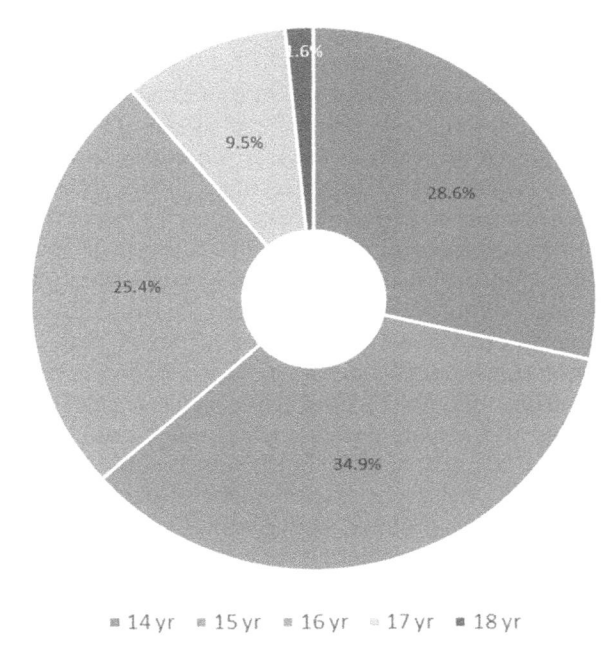

Fig. 7.6 Motivation: To feel wanted

As the reasons given by the participants did not indicate the elements of aggravated sexting, this factor was moved from the grouping Exploitation to that of Social Status. The distribution across the sub-category age range of the study shows that 65.7% of these occurrences were recorded by those boys aged 15 years and 16 years old.

Exploitation

Where the analysis of the motivational prompts that the study participants selected chose, those that fall within the category of exploitation showed the respective participant to be a victim of sexually harmful behaviour. This underlines the importance of not only looking at the 'what'—the content of the messages involved, but at the 'why'—the intent behind the event. The focus of this study was not to examine the aggravated, exploitative nature of sexting but it is necessary to analyse the results from the study and demonstrate, from a safeguarding perspective, so that those participants who disclosed an abusive situation were sufficiently protected and supported.

Hackett (2019) describes a continuum of sexualised behaviours ranging from what he describes as 'normal' behaviour to that described as 'highly deviant' in nature when looking at the intention behind sexually harmful behaviour. This continuum describes normal adolescent behaviours within a construct that is developmentally expected by age, social acceptability within a community and within a consensual, mutually reciprocal framework. From this start point, Hackett describes intention that drives behaviours starting with inappropriate behaviour. It can be argued that the domain of experimental sexting sits within the framework of the Hackett's continuum as a sexual behaviour that may be socially acceptable within a peer group but not accepted in a wider societal context. This demonstration of problematic behaviour may not include overt or intentional victimisation but may describe behaviours that may be developmentally appropriate but that are expressed inappropriately in each context such as an active sexting situation between participants of a similar age. Abusive behaviours involve an element of coercion or manipulation and a power imbalance due to age, aggressivity, intellectual ability, disability, or physical strength. Problematic and abusive sexual behaviours are developmentally inappropriate. Abusive sexual behaviour may or may not result in a criminal conviction or prosecution; however, the behaviour has potential to cause physical or emotional harm.

Whilst it has been demonstrated that sexting within a relationship may be beneficial, the motivations underpinning sexting with the intention to cause harm falls into three main categories; to share images as a means to exert social dominance; to coerce images from a partner against their will or, to exhort sexual content with criminal intent. Ojeda et al. (2019), García-Gómez (2019), and Setty (2019a, b) describe the practice of sexting to exert dominance over a social group either to demonstrate a perception of masculine identity or as a visual code of male regulation and control over those receiving the sext message. This negative motivational factor to cultivate a hierarchical dominant social standing has the potential to harm the recipient because of the coercive and controlling behaviours being exhibited by the sender.

This is a deviation away from curating images for personal use, to the unsolicited sharing of images and explicit text without request or consent from the recipient. This motivational factor, to cultivate a dominant social standing, where images of others are shared without consent, will lead to reputational harm for the victim but also has the potential to harm the sender, including through pejorative criticism and legal redress.

Kernsmith et al. (2018) in their study demonstrated that 20% of their teen sample reported being coerced into sexting by their dating partner. Paasonen et al. (2019) identify a negative impact on the sender as well if the images sent are not well received and result in criticism, body shaming, or lead to reputational harm where images are shared without consent.

Paasonen et al. (2019), amongst many other authors, describe the potential harm when images are supplied following coercion within a relationship. Dodaj and Sesar (2020, p. 19) write that within a relationship 'pressure often occurs in situations where one of the partners requires a person with whom she/he is intimate to send sexually explicit content' and they note that this is often interpreted by an unwilling partner as the price that is paid to maintain a relationship. García-Gómez (2019) notes that this practice may not demonstrate a motivation to intentionally harm the other person by a deliberate subjugation of the other, but that it is a demonstration of one partner putting their needs ahead of the other.

Medrano et al. (2018) outline a particular motivation to sext can be to gather sexual information or content through the acquisition of increasingly more explicit content, to initiate sex, or to extort money or goods, and define this as on-line sexual coercion and extortion of those under the age of 18 years.

Within the study underpinning this book there was little reported empirical evidence that pressure, or coercion was a key factor, motivating the self-production of nude and semi-nude pictures with only 1% of the responses recorded the motivation to participate as an aggravated reason. The subset choices available to the participants included sexting as a means to hurt or harm another, to produce sexual content for money, or were forced to do as part of coercive or grooming behaviours (Fig. 7.7—Motivation: Aggravated factors).

However, in-line with the ethical requirements of the study, where participants revealed their involvement in potentially illegal activity, albeit historical in nature, the participant was signposted to the appropriate child protection support in accordance with the safeguarding regulations of the local authority in which the host school was situated. In these instances where confidentiality had to be breached, the participant was kept fully informed and ongoing support was offered via the host Designated Safeguarding Lead within the boy's school.

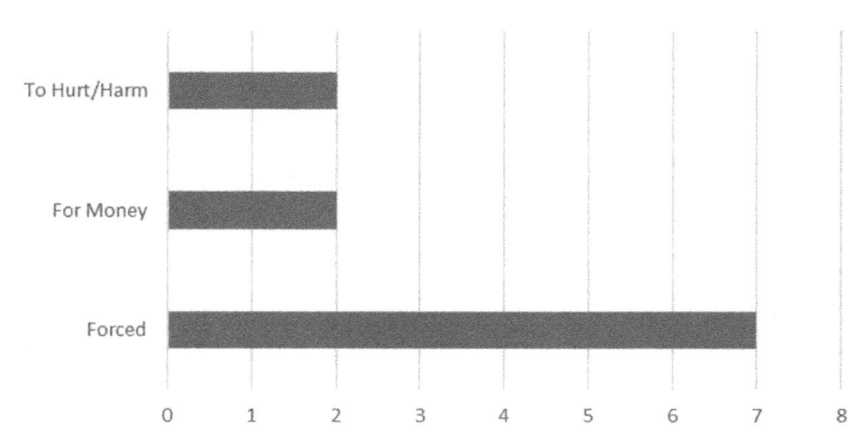

Fig. 7.7 Motivation: Aggravated factors

Participant Voices Against Sexting

During the analysis of the data, it became apparent that not all the free text comments were in support of sexting. 0.9% of those who were involved in both passive and active sexting expressed a negative reaction to the issue.

The major objection to sexting was raised on moral, or ethical grounds with 0.5% of participants declaring sexting to be either against their religious convictions or objecting to the potential for exploitation:

> I believe it is wrong to exploit a girl. (age 16)
> People do it out of peer pressure or the thought that one person. (age 15) wouldn't like them unless they show themselves in an explicit way.
> Sending nude pictures is inappropriate and bad. (age 15)
> I believe sexting is Haram and so against my religion. (age 14)

Neither within the sexting behaviour questionnaire or within the semi-structured interviews was the illegality of sexting mentioned other than if one party were an adult or there was a significant age gap.

Another objection raised related to the potential for participants increased interest in themselves or the need to protect themselves from exposure to any potential negative consequence:

> I would never send a photo of my bits because that's wrong. (age 17)
> I don't send pictures because I am focused on myself. (age 16)

This was specifically mentioned by 'James' in his interview, where he talked about the value he placed on himself and his relationships with others as being higher than his need to send explicit images:

> I don't think there is a time when it is acceptable. I have not ever sent any explicit images, but on the other hand I am a human being that doesn't need to show love by sending nudes. I show it through my personality and acts. (James, 14 years)

Finally, there were some comments that related to the impact previous sexting incidents had had upon the participants and their overall emotional health and wellbeing:

> After my pictures were shared I felt used and never really loved. I was broken and still feel ashamed for what I did…I was fooled. (age 17)
> It don't make you feel anymore loved. You shouldn't have to send stuff to feel that way. (age 14)

CHAPTER SUMMARY

This chapter has identified the four key motivational areas that prompt teenage boys to become involved in sexting. Sexual motivations prompted responses around flirting, arousal, and passion, with 76.1% of active sexts having a sexual purpose. Of those sexts relating to body image and attractiveness, 29.1% of the participants chose this motivation. A smaller number, 8.4% of participants, used sexting as a means to establish themselves within a social structure or friendship group. Finally, a very small proportion of reported incidents (1%) involved aggravated sexting where the intention to sext represented a safeguarding incident.

Not all the young people surveyed within the study supported the concept of sexting and raised moral or ethical objections based on their religious convictions, previous negative experiences, or objecting to the potential for exploitation.

For those working with educational provision to effect change in boys' behaviour, it is clear that the importance of understanding 'why' the boys are participating in sexting is more important than an operational response to 'what' they are sending and the sanctions that can be applied to alter actions.

The next chapter will consider what can be drawn from the results of the study the book is based upon. These will form two distinct sections; the first of these will offer a general discussion around what conclusions can be drawn and the second section looking at the specific recommendations for practice within schools, academies, colleges, and other educational settings.

REFERENCES

Albury, K. (2015). Selfies, sexts, and sneaky hats: Young people's understandings of gendered practices of self-representation. *International Journal of Communication, 9*, 1734–1745.

Albury, K. (2017). Just because it's public doesn't mean it's any of your business: Adults' and children's sexual rights in digitally mediated spaces. *New Media & Society, 19*(5), 713–725.

Bianchi, D., Morelli, M., Baioco, R., & Chirumbolo, A. (2017). Sexting as a mirror on the wall: Body esteem attribution, media models and objectified body consciousness. *Journal of Adolescence, 61*, 164–172.

Bianchi, D., Baiocco, R., & Morelli, M. (2016). Psychometric properties of the sexting motivations questionnaire for adolescents and young adults. *Rassegna di Psicologia, 3*(35), 5–18.

Bianchi, D. Morelli, M. Baioco, R. Chirumbolo, A. (2019). Individual Differences and developmental trends in sexting motivations. *Current Psychology* Published on-line.

Burén, J., & Lunde, C. (2018). Sexting among adolescents: A nuanced and gendered online challenge for young people. *Computers in Human Behavior, 85*, 210–217.

Casas, J., Ojeda, M., Del Elipe, P., & Ray, R. (2019). Exploring which factors contribute to teens' participation in sexting. *Computers in Human Behavior, 100*, 60–69.

Clancy, E., Klettke, B., Crossman, A., Hallford, D., Howard, D., & Toumbourou, J. (2021). Sext dissemination: Differences across nationals in motivation and associations. *International Journal of Environmental Research and Public Health, 18*(2429), 1–16.

Del Ray, R., Ojeda, M., Cassas, J., Mora-Merchán, J., & Elipe, P. (2019). Sexting among adolescents: The emotional impact and influence of the need for popularity. *Frontiers in Psychology, 10*(1828), 1–11.

Dodaj, A., & Sesar, K. (2020). Sexting categories. *Mediterranean Journal of Clinical Psychology, 8*, 2. Published online.

Foody, M., Kuldas, S., Sargioti, A., Mazzone A., & O'Higgins Norman, J. (2023). Sexting behaviour among adolescents: Do friendship quality and social competence matter? *Computers in Human Behavior, 142*, 1–8. ISSN 0747-5632.

Foody, M., Mazzone, A., Laffan, D., Loftsson, M., & O'Higgins-Norman, J. (2021). It's not just sexy pics' An investigation into sexting behaviour and behavioural problems in adolescents. *Computers in Human Behavior, 117*(106662), 1–8.

García-Gómez, A. (2019). Sexting and hegemonic masculinity: Interrogating male sexual agency. In P. Bou-Franch & B. Garecés-Conejos (Eds.), *Empowerment and Dominant Gendered Norms: New Insights and Future Directions* (pp. 313–339). Analyzing Digital Discourse.

Hackett, P. (2019). *Harmful sexual behaviour framework* (2nd ed.). NSPCC, UK. [online] Accessed 25/04/23, from https://www.icmec.org/wp-content/uploads/2019/04/harmful-sexual-behaviour-framework.pdf

Kernsmith, P., Victor, B., & Smith-Darden, J. (2018). Online, offline, and over the line: Coercive sexting among adolescent dating partners. *Youth & Society, 50*(2), 1–14.

Maheux, A., Evans, R., Widman, L., Nesi, J., Prinstein, M., & Choukas-Bradley, S. (2020). Popular peer norms and adolescent sexting behaviour. *Journal of Adolescence, 78*, 62–66.

McKie, R., Milhausen, R., & Lachowsky, N. (2016). Hedge you bets': Technology's role in young gay men's relationship challenges. *Journal of Homosexuality,* Published on-line, April, 1–20.

Medrano, J., Rosales, F., & Gámez-Guadix, M. (2018). Assessing the links of sexting, cybervictimization, depression, and suicidal ideation among university students. *Archives of Suicide Research, 22*, 153–164.

Morelli, M., Urbini, F., Bianchi, D., Baiocco, R., Cattelino, E., Laghi, F., Sorokowski, P., Misiak, M., Dziekan, M., Hudson, H., Marshall, A., Nguyen, T., Mark, L., Kopecky, K., Szotkowski, R., Van Demirtaş, E., Outsel, J., Voiskounsky, A., Bogacheva, N., Ioannou, M., Synott, J., Tzani-Pepelasi, K., Balakrishnan, V., Okumu, M., Small, E., Nikolova, S., Drouin, M., & Chirumbolo, A. (2021). The relationship between dark triad personality traits and sexting behaviours among adolescents and young adults across 11 countries. *International Journal of Environmental Research and Public Health, 18*(2526), 1–25.

Mowlabocus, S. (2007). Gay men and the pornification of everyday life. In S. Paasonen, K. Nikunen, & L. Soarenmaa (Eds.), *Pornification: Sex and sexuality in media culture* (pp. 61–71). Berg.

Needham, J. (2021). Sending nudes: Intent and risk associated with 'sexting' as understood by gay adolescent boys. *Sexuality & Culture, 5*(2), 396–416.

Ojeda, M., Del Rey, R., Ortega-Ruiz, R., & Casas, J. (2019). Sexting: A new way to explore sexuality. In F. Wright (Ed.), *Digital technology* (pp. 99–124). Nova Science.

Paasonen, S. Light, B., & Jarrett, K. (2019). The dic pic: Harassment, curation, and desire. *Social Media and Society*, April–June, 1–10.

Raine, G., Khouja, C., Scott, R., Wright, K., & Sowden, A. (2020). Pornography use and sexting amongst children and young people: A systematic overview of reviews. *Systematic Reviews, 9*(283), 1–12.

Reed, L., Boyer, M., Meskunas, H., Tolman, R., & Ward, M. (2020). How do adolescents experience sexting in dating relationships? Motivations to sext and responses to sexting requests from dating partners. *Children and Youth Services Review, 109*(104696), 1–10.

Ricciardelli, R., & Adorjan, M. (2018). If a girl's photo gets sent around, that's a way bigger deal than if a guy's photo gets sent around: Gender, sexting, and the teenage years. *Journal of Gender Studies, 28*(5), 563–577.

Sagrera, C., Magner, J., Temple, J., Lawrence, R., Magner, T., Avila-Quintero, V., McPherson, P., Alderman, L., Bhuiyan, M., Patterson, J., & Murnane, K. (2022). Social media use and body image issues among adolescents in a vulnerable Louisiana community. *Front Psychiatry, 13*, 1–14.

Setty, E. (2019a). 'Confident' and 'hot' or 'desperate' and 'cowardly'? Meanings of young men's sexting practices in youth sexting culture. *Journal of Youth Studies*, Published on-line, July, 1–17.

Setty, E. (2019b). A rights-based approach to youth sexting: Challenging risk, shame, and the denial of rights to bodily and sexual expression within youth digital sexual culture. *International Journal of Bullying Prevention*, Published on-line, November 19, 1–14.

Stanley, N., Barter, C., Wood, M., Aghtaie, N., Larkins, C., Lanau, A., & Överlien, C. (2018). Pornography, sexual coercion and abuse and sexting in young people's intimate relationships: A European study. *Journal of Interpersonal Violence, 33*(19), 2919–2944.

Van Ouytsel, J., & Dhoest, A. (2021). The prevalence, context, and perceptions of sexting among non-heterosexual men from various generations in Belgium. *Computers in Human Behavior, 126*. Published on-line.

Van Ouytsel, J., Ponnet, K., & Walrave, M. (2014). The associations between adolescents' consumption of pornography and music videos and their sexting behavior. *Cyberpsychology, Behavior and Social Networking, 17*(12), 772–778.

Van Oosten, J., & Vandenbosch, L. (2017). Sexy online self-presentation on social network sites and the willingness to engage in sexting: A comparison of gender and age. *Journal of Adolescence, 54*, 42–50.

Weisskirch, R., Drouin, M., & Delevi, R. (2017). Relational anxiety and sexting. *The Journal of Sex Research, 54*(6), 685–693.

CHAPTER 8

General Discussion, Conclusions, and Developments

Abstract This chapter explores the complex, overlapping motivations behind teenage boys' engagement in sexting, emphasising that these motivations are not singular but intersectional. These behaviours exist on a continuum from socially accepted adolescent expression to deviant acts, depending on context, consent, and community norms. Traditional educational approaches fail to address adolescent sexting, especially when driven by sensation-seeking and impulsivity. Simply condemning sexting reinforces control over sexual agency and ignores the nuanced, consensual experiences of teens. Approaches to education that conflate experimental and aggravated sexting, distort adolescent realities. An inclusive, critical RSE curricula that embrace diverse sexual discourses and promote ethical, informed decision-making through digital sexual literacy aligns with a call for sex education that reflects young people's lived experiences.

Keywords Consent • Curriculum development • Sexual ethics • Education policy • Harm reduction • On-line harm • Rights-based education • Sexting legislation

This text has investigated the motivations, behaviours, and the impact of sexting on adolescent males to address the perceived gendered double standard surrounding sexting. Whereas the majority of the published research and societal narrative focuses primarily on the impact sexting has on girls as promiscuous or victims, and for boys as a normalised behaviour, a joke, or as perpetrators of sexual crime. This limited stance risks restricting the male emotional response, openness and can present a duality between their own sexual experience and the expectations placed upon them by their social group.

This is not to detract from the important recognition that pressure, coercion, or problematic gendered practices occur as factors within some sexting practice as described by Setty et al. (2024) who address school-related sexual and gender-based violence. This book has examined the sexting behaviours of boys aged 14 years to 18 years old, including those who identify as heterosexual, homosexual, bisexual, those who are questioning their gender identity, and those youths in transition. Ricciardelli and Adorjan (2018, p. 570 & p. 572) describe this discounting of male emotional responses as 'culturally emasculating' and 'trivializing' their experiences, thus forcing teenage males to suffer in silence or risk violating the norms of socialised masculinities. Clarke et al. (2018) note that for young men that identify as gay, bisexual, transgender, or whose gender identity is 'other than heterosexual', the societal normative assumption further underestimates their response.

It is important that the lines of demarcation between the motivational options should not be seen as singular or absolute, rather as covariant, and intersectional. Obtaining approval for body shape and image could be a precursor to flirting with a partner as a means to initiate sex or an intimate relationship; sexting within a relationship may intersect with intentional or unintentional coercive behaviours, and the sending of images to a friend or group of peers could be an expression of identity, to create a sense of social cohesion or a form of behavioural reinforcement around a traditionally accepted view of masculinity.

Indeed, the intention behind a sexted message needs to be explored against a continuum of sexualised behaviours ranging from what may be described in different contexts as an expression of 'normal' behaviour within a broad social group to that described as 'highly deviant' in nature. This continuum describes normal adolescent behaviours within a construct that is developmentally expected by age, social acceptability within a community, and within a consensual, mutually reciprocated framework.

Albury (2017) identified that some images created by boys were an attempt to show muscle definition and could be posted on social media sites as an attempt to gain 'likes' and could be classified as boys seeking peer feedback about the adequacy of their body. However, Burén and Lunde (2018) write of the impact of sexting on the perception of self on body image and body dissatisfaction and suggest that this function be viewed as a tool by which adolescents explore and express sexuality as well as a measure of moderation and integration in their friendship groups. Therefore, the desire for boys to measure themselves against a perceived standard may well be conceived as an 'intention' but should also be considered as a motivation for engaging in the sharing of explicit images.

Curriculum Development

The argument that 'victims bring it upon themselves' has been refuted by campaigners in other key issues such as child sexual exploitation and rape, but continues to exist in educational resources addressing sexting, where responsibility is moved from those who share received images onto the victims who 'failed' to assure their own safety in an on-line environment. Unis and Sällström (2019, p. 4) identified that teenagers described the sex and relationship education received in schools as portraying sexuality as a problem to be managed and controlled is 'out of touch with many adolescents' lives'. This is similarly reflected in work by Katz and El-Asam (2019) which calls for more effective teaching within the relationships and sex education curriculum (RSE) that focuses on the real-life situations students face, and the skills and competencies to help them deal more effectively with arising situations. RSE Curriculum design should include a proportionate, zero-tolerance, and trauma-informed response to disclosures of sexual and gender-based violence (Setty et al., 2024, p. 436). Phippen and Brennan (2016, p. 3) identified that young people are asking for relevant teaching around on-line harm, and are 'calling for this intervention from an early age, and asking for educational spaces to provide a curriculum that addresses the concerns related to technology such as self-generation, on-line abuse and the influence of pornography, as well as more fundamental rights-based issues such as respect, consent, and privacy', this is echoed in work by Setty (2021, p. 3) who argues that young people 'require an education that speaks to their concerns and lived experience and legitimizes their sexual agency and subjectivities'. In acknowledging that sexting is likely to take place, it is necessary to focus on 'why it happens' rather than 'what it contains'. Maheux et al. (2020) report that teenagers were over ten times more likely to sext if they believed that the popular peers within their social group participated in sexting. Their work identified that boys were much more likely to be influenced by their peers, and therefore more likely to sext if they thought their male friends were also sexting.

Therefore, educational spaces need to move away from the gendered pedagogies of legality and shame, towards an ethical stance, in relation to both individual and collective expressions of sexual rights so that young people receive what Bragg et al. (2020) describe as a curriculum that delivers understanding, appropriate application to real life, and affirms the young person as an individual and also within their peer or social group. Similarly, Patchin and Hinduja (2020) are critical of an abstinence-based curriculum and advocate the use of a more comprehensive safe-sex curriculum that includes giving students knowledge to minimize risk if they participate in sexting behaviours. It is necessary to provide a relevant and current curriculum that reflects the requirements for age-appropriate content and references the need to proactively ensure that teachers, other adults, and parents are suitably educated in the 'real world' issues of sex, sexting, sexuality, and the cultural context faced by young people in their care.

Rosen et al. (2019) write that as influential social structures, schools, and academies play a pivotal role in the formation of attitude. They argue that the inclusion of the protected characteristic of gender identity is much less widespread. Rosen et al identified that a very small minority of students who identified as LGBTQ+ received positive messages about their lifestyle and instead learnt within a heteronormative curriculum. This is illustrated in work by Needham (2021, p. 413) who noted that the opportunity to marginalise gay issues continues to exist if adults do not recognise the divergent identities of their children. This point was illustrated with a participant quote from a semi-structured interview with 'Edward' a 14-year-old boy who commented on the lack of inclusion in the Relationship and Sex Education curriculum:

> *I think it is crucial that we get some appropriate gay role models, people who can say 'you are OK as you are.' And I think schools need to address the issue in their curriculum.* PHSE [Personal, Social and Health Education a British curriculum topic] *has been really difficult for me, the only mention of LGBTQ+ issues was last year when there was a sentence at the bottom of the page that said, 'at this age some people may have gay feelings, but this is usually just a phase'. This just left me cold; it didn't acknowledge my reality or my experiences and in fact belittled them. I don't think they should teach it in biology but definitely in PHSE.* (Edward, 14 years)

McKie et al. (2016) caution that unless educational settings provide an inclusive curriculum, students will seek advice from elsewhere. They note that for young gay men, the Internet affords an opportunity for an education filled with unrealistic expectations and learning that may offer sexual primacy over romance that will be in potential conflict with in-person situations and relationships. This view is supported by Lippman et al. (2023, p. 1205) who identify, as an example, the digital patronage platform 'OnlyFans' as a medium for sexual learning covering topics including 'sexual expression, sexual pleasure, sexual communication, and techniques to pleasure partners'.

A traditional approach to education and teaching practice will not meet the needs of an adolescent seeking sensation as well as impulsivity resulting in sexting behaviours and just calling for the cessation of sexting will not effect changes in a teenager's behaviour and actually only serves other performative strategies such as regulating sexual agency or sexual activity. Where the issues associated with aggravated sexting are conflated alongside the intent within experimental sexting, such as in the De Lonno report 'Not Just Flirting' (2022) where the lived experience of the adolescents who do sext within a consensual relationship is denied efficacy, when the 'adverse harm' message is repeated in pedagogical texts as though it were fact. Where the issues associated with aggravated sexting are conflated alongside the intent within experimental sexting, such as in the HM Government all-party parliamentary group publication (2021) the lived experience of the adolescents who do sext within a consensual relationship is denied efficacy and the 'adverse harm' message is repeated in pedagogical texts as fact. Mayo (2022, p. 654) calls for the RSE curriculum to incorporate a multiplicity of discursive elements to address a cultural hegemony and acknowledge a divide between a heteronormative dominant discourse and a different or contradictory paradigm. Rather, Setty (2020) argues that the discussions around digital sexual ethics need to be viewed alongside sexual literacy. Curriculum development and work with young people should encourage critical analysis in the context of their sexting practice. Setty argues that this will enable empowered ethical choices in terms of both themself and others.

Setty (2021) calls for a shift in focus in addressing behaviour, moving the blame attributed in sexting away from a victim blaming stance where the expectation is that any negative impact of sexting is the fault of the sender. Instead, the focus should be on the perpetrator of an aggravated sexting incident, who through lack of sufficient moral code, should not be trusted and punished as appropriate in line with the legal consequence of the country. To do otherwise, deflects attention away from the person who is obtaining sexts by coercion, bullying, and harassment.

Hypotheses Directing Behaviour

To understand the motivating factors that influence the sexting behaviours of teenage boys aged 14 years to 18 years, within the UK this book has postulated six hypotheses which are proposed as a framework for both the data analysis and as a means for educational establishments to begin to address sexting within their setting. These hypotheses include the demographic factors of age, ethnicity, faith structure, sexual orientation, access to and use of pornography, and relationship status and have helped develop a typology model against which educational spaces can begin to analyse and address the motivational characteristics of sexting.

Hypothesis One: The Older the Adolescent the More Likely to Sext

The first proposed hypothesis that the older the adolescent boy the more likely they are to participate in sexting, is supported through the data analysis. The presenting data for the average sexting rates of participants within the study, clearly show a year-on-year increase, by age, in active sexting. This was demonstrated by a 38.2% difference between 14- and 18-year-olds. The average active sexting of teenagers aged 14 years old was 39.2% compared to 77.4% of those aged 18-year-old.

The analysis of the passive message content shows that the sex messages were predominantly image based of either naked males or females. Explicit written material relating to females was almost exclusively received by those participants that identified as heterosexual, and conversely, explicit text messages relating to male sexual practices were received by those participants who identified with a homosexual, bisexual, transgender, or a gender diverse identity. All the participants reported receiving images of naked men, though 35.4% more were received by the gay, bisexual, and gender diverse participants, with the exception of topless images of men which were almost exclusively received by those who identified as 'other than heterosexual', with this potentially linked to the sexualisation of the male body without explicit content.

When comparing the content of the active messages, the data shows that as with active messages sent to a known recipient, the sext messages were predominantly image-based, with fully naked pictures being sent in almost equal measure by heterosexual, gay, bisexual, and gender diverse boys. Of the messages sent by the participants who identified as gay, bisexual, and gender diverse, 53.2% of these were predominantly naked images to strangers, and those boys who identified as heterosexual 44.2% were involved in also sending explicit messages and semi-naked images to people they did not know. Therefore, when looking at the content of active sexting messages through the lens of potential risk-taking behaviours, boys who send images to a stranger are potentially exposing themselves to a much higher level of risk.

The issues that arise from the existing legal restrictions around the attainment of legal majority and the age of consent, and identity development around the male teenage awareness of masculinity, gender, and sexual orientation. The combination of the reinforcement of misogyny in different youth subcultures and the potential impact of traditional male hegemonic narratives of female objectification and female passivity do not make it easy for educational settings to address sexting.

In addition, Van Dijke et al. (2025) note that most of the published lexicon attempts to frame the negative impact of sexting. Much of which defines negative issues as including poor self-esteem, negatively affected emotional health, and is linked to behaviours that impact on physical health, such as drug taking, alcohol consumption, and higher risk sexual practice. The literature assumes the issues of teen sexting and high-risk behaviours are potentially subject to other negative but variant factors. These factors include a lack of parental supervision, associating with delinquent peers, impulsivity, and a lack of life experience. Thus, sexting incidence linked to increasing age is seen to be associated with risk taking behaviours. However, the published literature does not take a definitive stance as to whether sexting is the cause of, or a symptom associated with, vulnerability.

Whilst there is a clear legal position around the age at which certain sexualised images cease to be illegal, there is a potential disconnect between the legal system and adolescent sexuality; where a teenage couple aged 16 and over, exercising their legal right to be sexually active, cannot record, photograph, or otherwise document their union, without breaking the law. When asked, many teenagers do not appreciate the interstice between the age of consent, the age of majority, and the creation and curation of sexual images.

Hypothesis Two: The Prevalence of Sexting Varies with Ethnicity

Comparison with the Office for National Statistics distribution and the distribution rates of this underpinning study shows no statistically significant differences in the data between the expected and observed percentages, showing a similar normal distribution rate between the two. This would indicate that the results displayed within this book are applicable to an interpretation across the wider society.

When analysing the study participants' sexting habits by ethnicity, it can be demonstrated that participants from a British Asian heritage participate in overall sexting less than their peers from a White British, Dual Heritage, or Black British background with a reported 9% difference in both active sexting rates between White British, and Asian Heritage teenage boys. However, when analysing the data of participants who have been in receipt of sexual messages as passive sexts within all ethnic groups, the results are broadly similar.

This second hypothesis therefore that 'the prevalence of sexting varies with ethnicity' is established when comparing sexters and non-sexters. Post-hoc non-parametric analysis clearly identifies that participants from a British Asian heritage participate in sexting significantly less when compared to their White British, Dual Heritage, or Black British peers. However, when examining the sexting practice of those active sexters the ethnicity of participants has both a limiting and limited impact on prevalence and practice on behaviour.

Rates by ethnicity show sexting to be a practice across all ethnic groupings within the UK, with a general rise in incidence between 2016 and 2022. In the first data drawn during 2016, boys from the Asian British communities had a prevalence rate significantly lower than other communities, the data from the 2022 data collection demonstrated a rise in sexting of 20% in the Pakistani boys and a 31% rise in Indian boys and a 30% rise those with an Arab heritage. This calls for further investigation into the impact of heritage and faith on sexting habits and the development of an overall generic British teenage identity rather than one shaped by ethnicity alone.

Hypothesis Three: Boys Who Identify as 'Other Than Heterosexual' Are More Likely to Sext

This study is grounded in a social constructionist approach that identifies separately biological sex and that of a social gender division. Whilst a biological definition allows an approach that is useful to measure the supposed 'naturalness' of gendered practices it does not address the poststructuralist definitions of gender dynamics of identity and the contextual variants that impact on individuality that may not relate to a gendered pattern. Recognising gender expression as a construct of sexual identity supports the axiological approach underpinning this book by asking the young people to define their gender and sexual orientation as they interpret it, measuring gender against three classes of sex-gender configuration. The first class is based upon a binary gender identity expressed by an individual, ranging from highly binary to highly 'queer'. The second class is based on non-binary satisfaction of sexual identity measured against the acceptance of a cis-like or gender diverse identity. The final classification of gender identity is based around an influencing definition as a 'real' man. This post-structural approach recognises the concepts of sexual identity to be open, fluid, and non-fixed and challenges the notion of categorising within a binary choice of either heterosexual or homosexual, but rather deconstructing both into the experience of the individual alongside an emerging cultural shift in sexual identity.

Both heterosexual and those participants who identified as 'other than heterosexual' reported receiving images of naked men, though by percentage, significantly more were received by the gay, bisexual, trans, and gender diverse participants. Again, semi-naked images of women were received by both groups of participants, but topless images of men were almost exclusively received by those who identified as 'other than heterosexual'.

When examining active sexting rates, 56.6% of teenage males who identified as heterosexual self-reported as active sexters. Of those participants who identified as 'other than heterosexual', 71.6% reported that they participated in active sexting. Of the messages sent by the participants who identified as gay, bisexual, and gender diverse, they almost all contained naked images predominantly sent to strangers rather than someone they knew in the off-line world.

In understanding the participants' reaction to sexting by gender identity and message content, the participants that identified as heterosexual and those that identified within the bisexual, gay, transgender, or gender diverse community, the patterns of response were quite different.

When the participants who identified as heterosexual were asked how they reacted to sexting messages, they received on a 5-point Likert scale from people they knew and someone that they did not really know. Their responses support the published literature, showing that with sext messages from a known person only a small percentage (6.7%) of respondents reported that they did not like or felt uneasy at receiving a passive message. Most teenage boys claimed that they were either not bothered or enjoyed receiving a sext message. In addition, when relating to received messages containing sexual content relating to men the majority (75%) of participants did not report adverse effect. There was an overall acceptance of male content as with content containing female images and messages. The proportion of boys responding as being 'not bothered' by receipt of these images and messages warrants the exploration of this detached indifference as it could be a response that indicates a sign of blunted affect or having become inured to such imagery if they are in continued receipt of such images.

In relation to those study participants who identified as bisexual, gay, transgender, or gender diverse and who had received passive sext messages with image content about females, a slightly higher percentage of the participants 'didn't like' receiving messages from a known source (9.5%) or an unknown source (12.5%) compared to their heterosexual peers, though the number who reported to be adversely affected by receiving such a sext was very small. However, the majority of bisexual, gay, transgender, or gender diverse participants reported being 'not bothered' by the female content (33.3% known source, 55% unknown source), with fewer (though still some) participants reporting that they were 'glad they had received the message' from both a known (9.5%) and unknown (10%) source with female content. This may be associated with an acceptance of their sexual identity and the lack of sexual desire attached to the female form.

Whilst receiving messages containing sexual content relating to women, the majority of gay, bisexual, transgender, and gender diverse participants were not adversely affected. In instances of receiving nude, semi-nude, and explicit messages from an unknown source, there was a marked increase in the enjoyment of messages received from known senders whether the message contained explicit material of males or females.

Clarke et al. (2018) note that for young men that identify as gay, bisexual, transgender, or gender identity as other than heterosexual, the societal normative assumption further underestimates their response and supports the call from Ricciardelli and Adorjan (2018, p. 577) that criticises the responses to sexting that are 'based on individual responses to atomistic circumstances instead of a broader sociological topography of digital sexual expression'.

Therefore, the hypothesis that boys who identify as 'other than heterosexual' are more likely to sext is conclusively proven in active sexting situations between known parties with a 15% difference between heterosexual and GBT+ active sexting to known recipients and confirmed in active sexting situations with a 9% difference between straight and gender diverse participants to unknown recipients.

Hypothesis Four: Boys Who Regularly Access Porn Are More Likely to Sext in Comparison to Peers with Lower Reported Usage

The fourth hypothesis explored was whether boys who regularly access pornography are more likely to sext compared against the behaviours of their peers. Fairburn's (1994) model of adolescent development argues that whilst boys have little insight into what drives their peers, they themselves are driven by maturational processes and the development of secondary sexual characteristics. This physical development when paired with the increased access the on-line world allows an increased consumption of explicit material for stimulation and information. This approach challenges the thinking that a boy's access to on-line images is directly influenced by a peer-normative pressure, (i.e., doing it simply because everyone else is), but instead makes more direct links to the stage-normative measure of physiological and psychological pubertal development. Pylypa (1998) argues for the Foucauldian assertion on the influence of biopower on the normalcy discourse and the social regulation of the perception of an acceptable physical body. A pan-European study (Stanley et al., 2018) argued that there is a discernible pattern that as teenagers got older their access to porn reduced once they were engaged in in-person sexual relationships. Their study showed that, despite England having the highest rates for sending and receiving sexually explicit messages, the reported access to pornography by boys in the UK was the lowest in the European participant countries.

In attempting to understand the motivation behind sexting practice, it is important to establish the impact that the use of pornography has on societal values and attitudes, how these inform the research and policy decisions, and why a boy may choose to access on-line explicit material other than to fulfil a biological drive. The argument exists that sexual conservatism has limited the development of sex education in schools and suggests that young people look to the Internet as an alternative source of information on sexual behaviours, and furthermore that a curriculum based within a heteronormative framework pushes young gay men to seek their sexual education on-line, exposing them to unrealistic expectations and perceptions about sex and relationships. The analysis of the sexting behaviours questionnaire within this study showed the rates of active sexting increase for those heterosexual participants who access pornography (30.3%) when compared to non-sexting peers (22.4%) and their gender diverse peers (33.3%) but only by small margins.

When examining the data around pornography measured against age and frequency of active sexting, the increase of boys self-limiting their occasional access to pornography as they mature from 14 years old to 18 years old was discernible, with a corresponding decreasing trend line among those boys who regularly access on-line pornography. The assumption can be drawn that the active sharing of nude and semi-nude images (as self-produced sexual imagery) satiates the sexual drive and needs of teenagers and negates the need to rely on on-line pornography as a masturbatory aid. One assumption that can be made is that for a teenage boy the use of active sexting to share nude images within a sexual relationship replaces the access to on-line explicit images found in pornography.

Therefore, the hypothesis that boys who regularly access pornography are more likely to be involved in active sexting compared to the behaviours of their peers is only partially supported. Whilst the rates of active sexting have been demonstrated to slightly increase in the population of boys who access pornography, the use of pornography regularly decreases as the engagement in the sharing of youth produced self-generated images increases within active sexting by age.

Hypothesis Five: Boys in a Relationship Are More Likely to Sext

Comments from the semi-structured interviews imply that the process of developing a relationship from general social interaction to an intimate relationship within the teenage years is mediated through technology, particularly mobile phones. The published research also presents the sharing of nude images and explicit messages as the new norm in teenage relationship behaviours, with sexting as a new way that sexuality is explored in young people, underpinning sexual activity. If it is accepted that self-generated images act as a form of self-expression, then the primary reason for the initiation of sexting is the perception amongst young people that the sharing of explicit images now forms a widespread part of romantic relationships.

The data from this study and book revealed that the ethnicity of the participants had an impact on the formation of relationships. That boys from a British Asian heritage were less likely to identify as being in a relationship than any other of the ethnic heritage groups within the study. The data demonstrates that being in a relationship significantly increases the likelihood of a participant's involvement in sexting. The trend analysis around the sexual identity of the participant follows a similar increase with age, except for those participants who identify as bisexual or gender diverse, where their rates of active sexting during a relationship are higher than the average. Therefore, the proposed hypothesis is supported.

Hypothesis Six: Boys with an Active Faith Are Less Likely to Sext

Islam, Judaism, and Christianity as faith structures, can act as biosocial models that can moderate physiological influences by relevant social variables. Each of these religions place a level of prohibition on sexual activity outside marriage, and this prohibition can be interpreted to include the sending of explicit images and messages between teenagers. The Qur'ān and the Bible both stress the importance of modesty and decency and include the looking at bodies as an impurity. Sexting as an extension of this would be prohibited. Therefore, within this study's interpretation of the Sesar et al. (2019) Motivational Determinants Model, faith becomes a contextual determinant where the cultural and social values of the religion would encourage adherents who practice their faith to refrain from engaging in sexting and to conduct themselves with respect and modesty.

Analysis of the data showed that for those participants who were brought up within a Muslim household or in a home where there is no faith structure, adherence to the family led beliefs or no belief is relatively stable across the study age range. For those boys who identified their upbringing within a Christian ethos, there was a downward linear trend with boys aged 14 following their family faith reducing significantly to the participants having the same faith as their parents by the age of 18. In exploring this apostatic disaffiliation from Christianity, it is important to examine this abandonment or renunciation within the broader context of embracing an opinion that is contrary to their families' stated religious beliefs. Analysis of the data showed a decline in boys identifying within the established Christian denominations. However, in boys who identify within an evangelical or Pentecostal expression of Christianity, there was a rising trend in their adherence to faith by age.

Similarly, for those boys who did not identify as having a religious faith structure influencing their lives, participation in active sexting within a relationship was only slightly higher than their peers. Whilst for those boys who identified within one of the denominations of Christianity, the difference between those in a relationship but who did not sext and those in a relationship who did, was a difference of 38%. For those boys who identified within a Muslim sect the difference between sexting within a relationship and not sexting was 52.7%, and for those boys who were followers of other faiths the difference was 30.5%. This would indicate that holding a religious belief structure and following a faith, both reduce the likelihood of boys being in a relationship during their formative teenage years, but when they are in a romantic relationship the involvement in active sexting is *on par* with the reported active sexting rates among peer norms.

It is proposed then that within the Abrahamic religions the view sexting outside the confines of marriage as a prohibited activity and analysis of the study data revealed a difference in the active sexting rates of those with a professed faith that were slightly lower than their non-believing peers. This was especially notable in those boys who are followers of Islam, where it would appear that faith acts as a larger influencing factor on a boy's sexting behaviour. Therefore, the data supports the hypothesis that boys with an active faith are less likely to sext than those who profess not to follow a faith.

General Summary

The intersection between the individual and contextual determinants and the motivational determinants were plotted against a conceptual model that allows for these motivational factors to be mapped against the individual cognitive characteristics that have a moderating and mediating impact on sexting behaviour. These determinants were divided into two categories. The first category was the individual characteristics which act on the motivation to participate in sexting, such as sex, age, and cognitive characteristics stemming from intimate relationships. The second category was the contextual determinants of participation in sexting that include the perception of the cultural and social values of faith, ethnicity, and the influence of pornography.

The text within this book demonstrates that sexting is frequently undertaken in the period of young adulthood, although the first exposure begins in early adolescence. A more positive attitude in young people towards this form of behaviour also contributes to participating in sexting. Further, the needs for exploring sexuality, developing sexual agency, and improving one's social status and social position in their peer group lead to an increase in the participation in exchanges of sexually explicit content.

This research identified that the levels of sexting reported by those boys who were in a relationship were higher than those boys who identified as single. Burén and Lunde (2018, p. 215) note the initiation of sexting by age and pubertal development when a romantic partner was involved. The implication suggests the effect of romantic involvement places expectations upon the boy which have a greater influence on sexting behaviours than the age of thorarche itself. Symons et al. (2018) write that young people who perceive their peers to be more sexually active, with sexting as a behavioural norm, are more likely to integrate sexting practice into their own sexual repertoire.

A young person's decision to participate may also be made to maintain an intimate relationship, attract attention, and/or prompt the romantic or sexual interest of a potential partner. Although some previous authors report sexting to be linked to risk, the results of this research would indicate that sexting is predominantly seen by adolescent males as an integral part of a sexual or romantic relationship. The influence of social values and culture also has an impact. The social context within which sexuality exists, as a spectrum of difference, and is no longer considered taboo in a contemporary universal youth culture, would appear to contribute to the willingness of an individual to participate in sexting within a normative framework around the developmental exploration of identity, sexuality, and intimacy.

Research Limitations

Despite the innovative nature of this study and its implications for research and practice, the study was subject to some limitations. The first and greatest issue is the reliance on students self-reporting their involvement in sexting. It is unknown to what extent the reported answers reflected actual behaviour or what they thought that the researcher wanted to hear.

Although the students were assured that their answers would be confidential, and the results anonymised, it is still possible that some of the responses reflect what they think are socially desirable answers.

The study relied on a broad measure of sexual self-disclosure around both sexual identity and sexual practice. The study was limited to those participants whose parents and carers assented to their sons' participation. This relied on the willingness of parents to engage in a request for consent and then the parents to agree to a study that explored their child's sexuality and sexual practice. Burén and Lunde (2018) note the restrictive limitations that a reliance on parental consent may have, particularly on research related to their child's sexual behaviour. Seeking consent as the lawful basis for data gathering under the General Data Protection Regulations (GDPR) (Guide to the UK General Data Protection Regulation, 2018), children over 13 years old are deemed as the owners of their data and are afforded the same data protection rights as adults and under UK law are required to provide their own consent. The potential dilemma relating to parental consent and increased risk of harm in accidentally 'outing' a participant was presented in the ethics submission. The need for participant consent was upheld in-line with Article 9 (2)(j) and Article 89 (i) of the GDPR regulation for consent for scientific purpose and with the appropriate safeguards in place, but a general waiver of parental consent was not implemented within this study in order to comply with ethics restrictions.

Comprehension of the Legal Age to Sext

There was confusion among the participants as to whether sexting is permitted in law. Increasing sexting rates suggested this, as did the semi-structured interviews several of which identified that there is a lack of understanding about age restrictions. Currently, the UK legislation and policy frames the issue of 'sexting' within a deviancy milieu, which aligns coercive, unwanted sexting behaviours in adolescence with risk, problematised activities, and negative impact behaviours with 'aggravated' sexting only. This legal position ignores the potential for 'experimental sexting' within dating and/or romantic relationships as part of adolescent sexual self-expression.

In the UK as in many other countries, whilst the age of adult majority is assumed at 18 years old, the age of consent to sexual activity is 16 years old. However, the images involved in sexting of those under 18 years old are dealt with in UK law through the Protection of Children Act 1978 and the Criminal Justice Act 1998, where such images are considered images of child abuse. Therefore, the making of, distribution and storage of such images are dealt with under legislation as child protection issues, even when the images are self-generated and shared within a romantic relationship where both participants are over the age of consent to participate in a sexual relationship. The UK legal position remains that adolescent participation in sexting cannot be consensual, only abusive, and therefore requires legal intervention.

When asked in the semi-structured interviews, only 35% of the interviewees were able to articulate the legally allowed age for sexting. The larger proportion of 55%, conflating the age of consent and the legal age to sext, or justifying why they felt it was appropriate to break the law.

> OK, so I know I am going to get this wrong, but I think it is 16 years old. (Steve, 16 years)

> I think it should be the same as the age of consent, not if that means you're putting the age of consent up to 18 but lowering the age for images to 16 – I think that equalizing them to the age of 16 is the right way. (Edward, 16 years)

> I gather that it is 18 years old, but if you are 17 what is going to stop you, it should be between a couple in a relationship and set around 16 yrs. If you are sending it to another 16 yr. old then that is ok, if there was a 1-year gap I don't see an issue over 16. (Evelyn, 16 years)

A change in statute and legal intervention that harmonised the age of consent with the right to create and send self-generated images or sexual content within a consensual relationship over the age of 16 years would shift the focus away from the person sending the picture, commonly known as 'victim blaming'. This would enable law enforcement to identify the persons coercing images and sharing without consent and with criminal intent, as a way of 'perpetrator shaming' and supporting appropriate prosecution. Currently legal action relating to the non-consensual sharing of images, colloquially known as 'revenge porn', is restricted in UK law to those over the age of 18 years. Introducing parity in the age of consent to sexual activity and sexting would allow access to legal recourse where images were shared without consent for those teenagers between the ages of 16–18 years where coercion or sharing images without consent occurs. Until this change in the law happens, repeated studies need to explicitly state the age of consent and the legal age for permissible sexting.

REFERENCES

Albury, K. (2017). Just because it's public doesn't mean it's any of your business: Adults' and children's sexual rights in digitally mediated spaces. *New Media & Society, 19*(5), 713–725.

Bragg, S., Ponsford, R., Meiksin, R., Emmerson, L., & Bonell, C. (2020). Dilemmas of school-based relationships and sexuality education for and about consent. *Sex Education: Sexuality, Society & Learning*, Published on-line June 1–15.

Burén, J., & Lunde, C. (2018). Sexting among adolescents: A nuanced and gendered online challenge for young people. *Computers in Human Behavior, 85*, 210–217.

Clarke, K., Cover, R., & Aggleton, P. (2018). Sex and ambivalence: LGBTQ youth negotiating sexual feelings, desires, and attractions. *Journal of LGBT Youth*, published online, June, 1–16.

Fairbairn, W. (1994). Theoretical contributions to Object relations theory. In D. Shariff & E. Fairbairn-Birtles (Eds.), *From instinct to self; Selected papers of WRD Fairbairn, Volume 1 Clinical and theoretical papers* (pp. 200–264). E-book 2021, International Psychology Institute.

Katz, A., & El Asam, A. (2019). *In their own words: The digital lives of schoolchildren*. Internet Matters.org, London.

Lippman, M., Lawlor, N., & Leistner, C. (2023). Learning on onlyfans: User perspectives on knowledge and skills acquired on the platform. *Journal of Sex and Sexuality, 27*, 1203–1223.

Maheux, A., Evans, R., Widman, L., Nesi, J., Prinstein, M., & Choukas-Bradley, S. (2020). Popular peer norms and adolescent sexting behaviour. *Journal of Adolescence, 78*, 62–66.

Mayo, C. (2022). Gender diversities and sex education. *Journal of Philosophy of Education, 10*(1111), 1467–9752.

McKie, R., Milhausen, R., & Lachowsky, N. (2016). Hedge you bets': Technology's role in young gay men's relationship challenges. *Journal of Homosexuality*, Published on-line, April, 1–20.

Needham, J. (2021). Sending nudes: Intent and risk associated with 'sexting' as understood by gay adolescent boys. *Sexuality & Culture, 5*(2), 396–416.

Patchin, J., & Hinduja, S. (2020). It is time to teach safe sexting? *Journal of Adolescent Health, 66*, 140–143.

Phippen, A., & Brennan, M. (2016). The new normal? *Young People, Technology & Online Behaviour*. Accessed March 3, 2023, from https://www.nota.co.uk/

Pylypa, J. (1998). Power and bodily practice: Applying the work of Foucault to an anthropology of the body. *Arizona Anthropologist, 13*, 21–36.

Ricciardelli, R., & Adorjan, M. (2018). If a girl's photo gets sent around, that's a way bigger deal than if a guy's photo gets sent around: Gender, sexting, and the teenage years. *Journal of Gender Studies, 28*(5), 563–577.

Rosen, N. Peralta, R., & Merrill, M. (2019). Learning how sexual minorities in school and at home: How critical pedagogy can challenge heterosexism. *Cogent Education.*

Sesar, K., Dodja, A., & Šimić, N. (2019). Motivational determinants of sexting: Towards a model of integrating the research. *Psihologijske Teme, 28*(3), 461–482.

Setty, E. (2020). *Risk & harm in youth sexting culture – young people's perspectives.* Routledge.

Setty, E. (2021). Speaking the unspeakable: Education about youth digital intimacies in schools. *Academia Letters*, Article 483.

Setty, E., Ringrose, J., & Hunt, J. (2024). From 'harmful sexual behaviour' to 'harmful sexual culture': Addressing school-related sexual and gender-based violence among young people in England through 'post-digital sexual citizenship'. *Gender and Education, 36*(5), 434–452.

Stanley, N., Barter, C., Wood, M., Aghtaie, N., Larkins, C., Lanau, A., & Överlien, C. (2018). Pornography, sexual coercion and abuse and sexting in young people's intimate relationships: A European study. *Journal of Interpersonal Violence, 33*(19), 2919–2944.

Symons, K., Ponnet, K., Walrave, M., & Heirman, W. (2018). Sexting scripts in adolescent relationships: Is sexting becoming the norm? *New Media & Society, 20*(10), 3839–3857.

Unis, B., & Sällström, C. (2019). 'Adolescents' conceptions of learning and education about sex and relationships. *American Journal of Sexuality Education*, Published On-line, June, 1–28.

Van Dijke, S., Van den Eynde, S., & Enzlin, P. (2025). The bright side of sexting: A scoping review on its benefits. *Computers in Human Behavior, 164*, 108499. https://doi.org/10.1016/j.chb.2024.108499

CHAPTER 9

Recommendations for Educational Settings

Abstract This chapter critiques current UK educational guidance on sexting, particularly a framework, which only distinguishes between "experimental" and "aggravated" sexting. This binary approach overlooks the complexity of adolescent motivations. The chapter introduces the Four Motivation Options Typology for Boys (4MOTB), a model that maps the interconnected reasons behind sexting, ranging from romance to social validation, within a developmental and safeguarding context. It argues for a shift from punitive, absolutist approaches to a curriculum-based, harm-reduction strategy that reflects real life adolescent experiences. Sexting should be addressed through relationship and sex education (RSE) that supports ethical decision-making and acknowledges teenage sexual agency. The model encourages educators to assess each sexting incident individually, balancing legal obligations with developmental understanding. Educational settings need to deliver a progressive, evidence-based curriculum that moves beyond moral panic, empowering boys to critically reflect on their actions and make informed, ethical choices in digital sexual interactions.

Keywords Curriculum delivery · Cyber safety · Digital rights · Education policy · School Guidance · Harm reduction · Safeguarding · Typology model

Within this final chapter, it is the intention to make recommendations for practice, particularly within educational settings, to enable a more effective response to sexting activity. Firstly, the intention is to describe a new typology model based on motivation rather than message content. This new approach will allow practitioners to address the reasons behind the sext message when discussing the event with those involved.

Given the increased prevalence of sexting, it will then be proposed that a change in the delivery of sex and relationship education is required that addresses the needs of the young people and so reflects the reality of practice.

Finally, making changes to practice requires the issues of sexting to be addressed through changes to policy-and-practice, and so this chapter suggests how this could happen at a local and national level to support those professionals working with young people to offer the appropriate pastoral support and guidance within a statutory framework.

Typologies

To enable professionals to respond appropriately to incidents of sexting, several models of classification have been developed. These typologies are often grounded in the paradigm of sexting as risk rather than normative behaviour. As previously identified, models are often based within criminal definitions based on the Combating Paedophile Information Network in Europe (COPINE) Scale (Kloess et al., 2019), Luxembourg Guidelines (2016), image content derived from prisoner sentencing guidelines (UK All-Party Parliamentary Group, 2021), or criminal intent (Wolak & Finkelhor, 2011; Elliott & Beech, 2013), and focus on criminal intent and abuse. These typologies do not easily distinguish between the initial image content created within the context of a relationship between consenting teenagers from content featuring young children; and the motivation for generation of benign content and the further use being made of images with the intent to harm.

The 2020 United Kingdom Council for Child and Internet Safety (UKCCIS) provide guidance for UK schools dealing with 'sending nudes' but within a definition that does not fully address the issues of other content type. This seminal education guide identifies two main categories of nude image, based upon a study by Wolak and Finkelhor (2011). Their typology was developed after examining the criminal intent behind image sharing within legal cases that had come to the attention of the US judicial system. The model identifies incidents within an 'experimental' modality; youth generated images circulated to another young person to further romance, fun, or entertainment, and 'aggravated' images created or coerced with malicious intent. The UKCCIS guidance then directs schools to address experimental sexting incidents in-house, or for aggravated incidents by referral to the police. However, Dodaj and Sesar (2020) argue that the motivation to sext is influenced by contextual variables that need to be considered within a broader typology model. They argue that these variables include intimate relationship variables, flirting, or the desire to gain intimacy in relationship, demographic variables such as age, sex, gender, and cognitive variables such as personal attitudes towards sexting, perception of self-image, social status, and peer pressure. These variables will all have an impact on motivation, and they need to be considered when classifying and then addressing sexting incidents.

Identifying Four Motivational Factors to Sext

This book has positioned sexting predominantly within a normative framework of adolescent development within romantic and/or sexual relationships (Reed et al., 2020; Needham, 2021), and the likely motivational factors behind the desire to sext having been explored. Understanding the motivation behind the action of sexting may identify ways in which support to young people can be provided. If sexting is addressed with a broader, relevant curriculum relating to adolescent education and development then support can also be undertaken to address the prevention of abuse through focused intervention and support, including relationship education.

The analysis of the responses within this study classified the motivational determinants for an adolescent boy who has engaged in the sending of explicit material into four main motivational factors:

- Sexting to initiate sex or enhance romance.
- Sexting to seek external validation of body image.
- Sexting to increase social status and standing.
- Sexting with intent to cause harm.

Using the voice of the teenagers themselves has allowed a typology model to be developed that, whilst still viewed through the lens of safeguarding, allows each of these motivational areas to be paired with an appropriate policy approach. This allows educational settings to support teaching and pastoral staff who are required to deal with these incidents.

The lines of demarcation between the motivational options should not be seen as singular or absolute, but rather as covariant. Obtaining approval for body shape and image could be a precursor to flirting with a partner as a means to initiate sex or a relationship. The sending of images to a friend or group of peers could be an expression of identity, to create a sense of social cohesion, or represent a form of coercive behavioural control that acts as a reinforcing endorsement of a traditionally accepted, but potentially outdated (or at least contested) view of masculinity.

Sexting to Initiate Sex or Enhance Romance

If the revisionist discourse of sexting within adolescent relationships is accepted, then the management of incidents when reported to the school authorities should be addressed within a framework of sex and relationship education. Ojeda et al. (2019) place the responsibility to educate about sexting as a fundamental responsibility of schools. Integrating sext education into discussions around the use of technology and the ethics of normalising the role of sexting, whilst promoting harm reduction and safety strategies would move the issue away from a fear-based curriculum. In a study by Jørgensen et al. (2018), young people themselves asked for lessons based on the reality of life, and this was echoed by Katz and El Asam (2019) who reported that young people wanted education that delivered 'concrete help and advice to cope with real life situations'. The conclusion can be drawn that a school that does not have a comprehensive, fully inclusive approach to sex and relationship education based in the reality of the teenage lived experience may put their pupils at increased risk.

However, Walrave et al. (2014) note that whilst sexting within a relationship may be beneficial, the potential for coercion of images, pressure to provide images against an individual's better judgement, or the feeling that not sending sexts may end the relationship, can place undue pressure on a person, and would move sexting into a non-consensual domain.

Sexting to Seek External Validation of Body Image

Within a school setting, addressing the motivation to sext to gain an understanding of body shape, to seek validation around physical norms, or to celebrate muscular development, could be most meaningfully addressed through the curriculum. The Personal, Social, Health Education (PHSE) guidance (Great Britain. Department for Education, 2024) requires the need to understand physical and pubertal development to be addressed by age and within the curriculum delivered by the end of Key Stage 2 (11 years old), but this is not revisited again within the curriculum as the focus within Key Stage 3 focuses then on reproduction. Therefore, for the majority of young teenage boys, their understanding of puberty is theoretical and relies on their memory of lessons taught in primary school to understand the development of secondary sexual characteristics when it happens.

If the curriculum delivery within Key Stage 3 (age 12–14 years) were to offer a recap of pubertal development, the need to seek validation of body development through the sharing of images would be reduced. Similarly, giving a young teenager an evidence-based, realistic view of body development would reduce the need to seek 'education' from the Internet and pornography sites, helping to reduce the potential for unrealistic body shape expectations.

Sexting to Increase Social Status and Standing

Within an educational setting, addressing the motivation to sext to gain social status and standing with a peer group should be addressed through a robust inclusion strategy. Such a strategy would address the formation of social groups by ensuring that marginalised individuals and sub-groups are recognised, and their needs catered for. Creating a community within a setting such as a school that accepted and validated the individual regardless of their race, gender, sexual orientation, or belief structure, would go some way to mitigate against the need to share images to feel a sense of belonging within a community.

Setty (2019a, b) noted that some instances of sexting were perceived as 'jokes and banter' between friendship groups and that the social construct of masculinity was reinforced when images shared between male friends focused on what they 'look like' in terms of body shape and penile aestheticism rather than a focus on the fact they have shared a naked image.

Hertlein et al. (2015) write that this identification with a like-minded gay community can be seen to promote self-esteem and a sense of belonging to a group that otherwise feel marginalised by the comparison to a traditional hegemonic view of masculinity and therefore risk is mitigated by the sense of community and cohesion of belonging to a defined group.

'Queer community ethics, then, rely on a sense of sexual camaraderie and generosity that acknowledges a shared capacity to experience both public and private sexual indignities and embarrassments' (Albury, 2017, p. 720).

Alongside this approach to inclusion, should sit a strong behaviour policy that identifies what would be seen as acceptable and unacceptable behaviour in terms of legality. The principles of practice within such a policy would act as a driver for change by developing a relational culture, which recognises the transformative power of relationships to build belonging for young people within a safe and secure environment.

Sexting with Intent to Cause Harm

Within a typology model, the motivation underpinning sexting with the intention to cause harm falls into three main categories; to share images as a means to exert social dominance; to coerce images from a partner against their will; or to exhort sexual content with criminal intent.

The demarcation between sexting as an increasingly normal act within the developing adolescent's sexual agency and with intent to harm is one that is easily crossed. The intent to obtain or share images and sexual information to intimidate or harm another with malicious intent must be viewed as forms of sexual harassment and sexual violence and dealt with under a setting's statutory safeguarding procedures. This would result in a referral to, and investigation by the police, and dealt with through the legal process of child protection and prosecution of the perpetrators regardless of their age.

Sexting and Policy Development Within Education

In a study by Jørgensen et al. (2018), young people themselves asked for lessons based on the reality of life, and this was echoed by Katz and El Asam (2019, p. 32) who reported that young people wanted education that delivered 'concrete help and advice to cope with real life situations'.

Within educational settings, addressing the motivation to sext should be done through the lens of safeguarding and developmentally appropriate actions, but addressed through robust process, policy, and practice that identifies what would be seen as acceptable and unacceptable behaviour prompting the need to identify the key motivational factors within the stages of a relationship, with sexting as antecedental to intercourse or a new romance relationship.

It is clear then that an educational setting needs to address the four motivational domains that underpin sexting behaviours. If then the revisionist discourse of sexting within adolescent relationships is accepted, then the management of incidents when reported to the school authorities should be addressed within a framework of sex and relationship education. Hilton et al. (2024) and Ojeda et al. (2019) place the responsibility to educate about sexting as a fundamental responsibility of schools. Integrating sext education into discussions around the use of technology and the ethics of normalising the role of sexting, as well as promoting safety strategies moves the issue away from a fear-based curriculum.

Subjective judgements around self-identity, body image, and perceived attractiveness and appropriateness of body image need to be addressed through a school based, comprehensive, fully inclusive approach to sex and relationship education. This focus is especially important from early adolescence to young adulthood as the need to define 'normal' pubertal development challenge a young teenage boy's perception of general and sexual attractiveness. To not address 'normal development' at this age may put pupils at increased risk as they seek to find answers from alternative, unregulated sources.

Where sexting incidents occur as a means to fit into a social group then schools have a responsibility to promote inclusion. Whilst 'banter' between friends may seem innocent, it is crucial that school policy addresses both the expected values and behaviours of its pupils and offers an inclusive environment where everyone feels that they can thrive and belong. The challenge faced by schools related to the general applicability of sex and relationship (RSE) and personal, social, and health education lessons is to deliver a curriculum that incorporates the lived experiences of all students including those within gender and sexual minorities, rather than defaulting to a heteronormative narrative.

Guidance to UK schools is very clear, that incidents of experimental sexting should be addressed in-house whilst episodes of aggravated sexting should be referred to the police. Whilst the focus of this book was not to examine the aggravated, exploitative nature of sexting, it is clear that incidents should be dealt with through the lens of a safeguarding and child protection policy to ensure that any young people affected by child-on-child abuse or incidents of grooming by external sources are sufficiently protected and supported.

Four Motivation Options Typology for Boys

Using these four motivational areas, a graphical representation of a Four Motivation Options Typology for Boys (4MOTB) that shows the interconnected nature of the motivational areas and how national guidance, and local policies and process can support intervention where necessary. At the heart of this new model is the sexting episode defined by the widest characterisation including images, self-made media, text, recorded messages, and line drawings.

The application of this proposed model requires an assessment of any potential safeguarding issues surrounding each reported sexting episode to ensure that any aggravated situations are addressed. However, if there are no safeguarding concerns, then the model advocates addressing the sexting event through either a curriculum-based intervention or as part of relationship advice supported by an appropriate strategy to ensure that a balance is maintained between the application of the law and the acknowledgement of the development of teenage sexuality and the right to a private life.

By understanding the single or multiple motivational factors that prompted the sext, those exploring the sexting episode with the adolescent, have access to more effective policy and strategy-based solutions to allow them to determine the issues involved, and arrive at a workable solution for intervention and support (Fig. 9.1—Four Motivation Options Typology for Boys).

Any intervention delivered needs to be cognisant of the potential for multiple motivational factors and that behaviours can shift subtly into a situation that has the potential to harm one or both parties involved. If this is the case, then the sexting event acquires the status of something that demands institutional attention as part of a safeguarding response and the index incident viewed within a deficit context. What must not get lost within a statutory intervention is the prevalence of the behaviour, therefore the assessment and intervention should be dynamic to meet any developing needs.

Rights-Based Approach

In the UK, as in many other countries, whilst the age of majority is assumed at 18 years old, the age of consent to sexual activity is 16 years old. However, images involved in sexting are dealt with in UK law through the

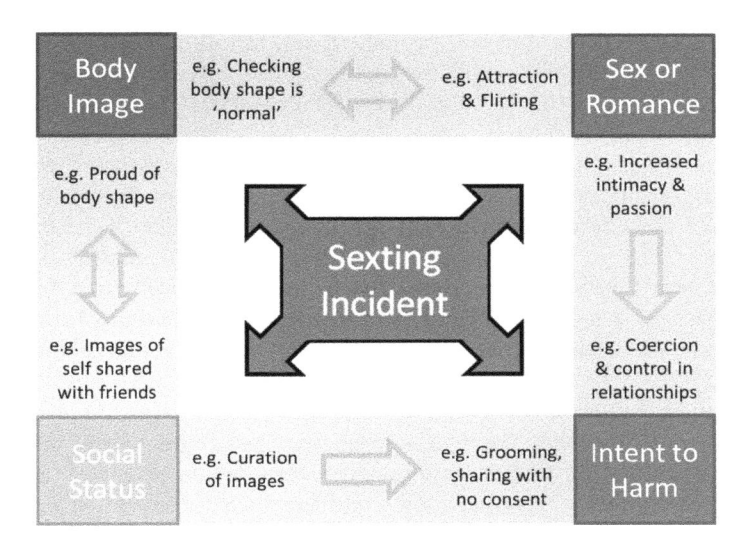

Fig. 9.1 Four motivation options typology model for boys

Protection of Children Act 1978 and the Criminal Justice Act 1998, where images of those under 18 years old are dealt with as child abuse, with a similar legislative stance being taken in many other countries' legal systems.

The argument put forward then is that the age at which sexting should be considered legal should be reduced from 18 years to 16 years when the images are made by young people under the age of 18 years. This would take into consideration the high rates of relationship based, consensual sexting in teenagers aged 16–18 years, and have a positive impact on the number of inappropriate referrals to the police for experimental sexting episodes. A reduction in the classification would also enable access to the law for prosecution following the sharing of images and messages colloquially known as the 'revenge porn legislation' that is currently only applicable over the age of 18 years old.

This shift away from a strictly legalistic approach to one based more on the digital rights of the young person is supported within the United Nations (UN) Convention on the Rights of the Child (1989). This charter promotes the teenager's right to access information and to self-expression; the intent being for minors to become active citizens, their

Rights must be promoted and protected, and the child must understand them. The UN Convention promotes the right to increasing capacity with age (article 5), the right to freedom of expression (article 13), and the right to privacy (article 16).

However, as Albury (2017) identifies, the UN Convention provides potential internal conflicts when teenagers' self-expression and their sexual rights are considered. Article 3 of the Convention talks of actions that must be taken in the best interest of the child and Article 34 of a Government's duty to protect children from all forms of sexual exploitation. The optional protocol to the Convention on the Rights of the Child on the sale of children, child prostitution, and child pornography (2011) makes reference to all images of children under the age of 18 but does not differentiate between those self-generated within experimental sexting and those images made for exploitation. If all sexting is viewed as 'child abuse' then the Convention requires protection for its victims. If sexting, without coercion or exploitation, by teenagers for teenagers, is seen as a recognition of sexual rights within a freedom of expression, then conflict with the Convention occurs.

Setty (2019a, b) argues that the response to sexting by professionals working with young people could appear to reverse a teenager's right to privacy when dealing with the sharing of sexting incidents. Often the responsibility for a breach in privacy is blamed on the person sending the message, rather than the person circulating the message to others. They comment on the narrative that states the risks of sexting are well known and to avoid the wider circulation of images they should not be shared in the first instance. This argument ignores the concept of sexting within a stable and loving relationship and shifts the blame to the victim, which creates 'an appealing narrative that simple common-sense rules of risk reduction can prevent on-line victimisation...regulating and controlling the potential victim's behaviour – rather than the potential assailant – is often an ineffective strategy that implies sexual assault is inevitable' (Hasinoff, 2015 p.59).

Recommendations

In conclusion then, the recommendations to enable a change to the professional response of staff working with young people in educational settings and beyond to address the issues of sexting at a local and national level, fall into three main areas:

Recommendation One: Introduction of New Typology

The adoption of the 4MOTB typology model that acknowledges the 'why' a teenage boy would participate in sexting, in its fullest description, incorporating nude and semi-nude images, messages, video content, and line drawings, rather than a classification system that identifies the 'what' of the image-based content. Using a model that looks at the motivation of sexting, enables a review of policies that underpin a statutory framework of practice and can apply a direct influence on the practitioner's approach to appropriate pastoral support and guidance.

A curriculum that delivers personal, social, health, and economic (PSHE) lessons that incorporates an unbiased approach to the purpose, benefits, and risks associated with sexting into the lesson plans will enable young people to hear an 'in real life' account of the pressures faced by teenagers. Similarly, an inclusion strategy that recognises, celebrates, and validates the individual will address the adolescent need to fit into a wider group identity and social faction.

Acknowledging the widespread involvement of sexting in teenage relationship scripts is crucial to change. Addressing sexting either as an aid to sexual intimacy or as part of a new or established relationship within the curriculum delivery of relationships and sex education (RSE) will help to address the developing agency of those involved. Where sexting practice shifts from the experimental to aggravated in nature, the delineation between supportive practice and disciplinary intervention will be clear. This will allow clearly identified support for the victim and targeted intervention for the perpetrator.

Recommendation Two: Rights Not Rules

To date, legislation and policy has framed the issue of 'sexting' within a deviancy framework, which aligns coercive, unwanted, aggravated sexting behaviours in adolescence, with risk and problematised activities, whilst ignoring the potential for 'experimental sexting' within dating and romantic relationships as part of a healthy form of adolescent sexual self-expression.

The current application of the law identifies that the sharing of nude images of young people under the age of 18 is illegal. However, the wider definition of sexting to include written messages, voice notes, and line drawn pictures, is not addressed in the legislation, nor is there a clear definition of 'indecency' in the law. The College of Policing briefing note issued in 2016 cautions against the criminalising of those under 18 involved in self-generated images or images obtained with consent by other teenagers, calling instead for a proportionate response. This 'outcome 21' response allows the acknowledgement that a whilst crime has been committed, formal action against the teenager is not in the public interest.

Whilst the age of adult majority is assumed at 18 years old, the age of consent to sexual activity is 16 years old, images of those under 18 years old involved in sexting are currently dealt with in UK law as images of child abuse. Therefore, the making of, distribution and storage of such images are addressed under legislation as child protection issues, even when the images are self-generated and shared within a romantic relationship where both participants are over the age of consent, but which cannot be legally defined as consensual, only abusive, and therefore requires legal intervention. It is a recommendation that harmonising the age of consent with the right to create and share self-generated images or sexual content by consensual agreement between participants aged 16 to 18 years old should occur. This action will bring parity to the age of consent for sexual activity and the age at which an image is deemed to be of a child to those under 16 years old and help reduce the confusion felt by young people. It will also reduce the labelling of young people involved in experimental sexting as criminals. This action will also allow police forces to focus on the aggravated episodes of sexting where coercion or sharing images without consent has occurred.

Recommendation Three: Harm Reduction Within Curriculum Delivery

It is clear from the data within this book that the sexting rates in boys aged 14–18 years have increased despite the education, legislation, and curriculum delivery in schools. The study revealed through its key findings that:

- Access to passive sexting and the involvement in active sexting is happening earlier in a young boy's development.
- Active sexting is predominant in relationships.
- Sexting between those boys who do not identify as heterosexual is higher than their cis-gendered peers.
- Sexting between teenage boys and unknown persons happens and is increasing.

In light of these findings, it is recommended that the delivery of curriculum materials around sexting represents the sex positive, real-life experiences of young people. The traditional approach to a sexting education pedagogy has been demonstrated not to meet the needs of a teenage boy seeking sensation as well as impulsivity that results in sexting behaviours. Where an absolutist approach that promotes cessation of sexting will not effect changes in a teenager's behaviour, Hilton et al. (2024) argue that a curriculum that encourages learning targeted specifically at the learning styles of boys will have more impact on the teenage boy's control of his own actions.

Phippen and Bond (2023, p. 111) advocate that a curriculum should address sexting within a harm reduction methodology that acknowledges the teenage boy's lived experience and delivers appropriate application to real life situations. They advocate that the potential for change, in those who wish to engage with 'a more progressive approach… the need for policymakers to move away from moral panic and judgement of the upcoming generation and instead learn from the evidence base and authentic youth voice'.

It is argued that for a curriculum intervention to be effective, it should acknowledge that sexting is going to happen and so should be undertaken safely with the minimum exposure to harm and risk. The relationship and sex education lessons should incorporate discursive elements to address a divide between the heteronormative dominant discourse and contradictory paradigms so that students who identified as LGBTQ+ receive positive messages about their lifestyle so as to affirm each young person as an individual and also their place within their peer or social group. Further, Phippen and Bond (2023) write about five key elements to a curricular approach of harm reduction:

- The importance of speaking to young people, listening to and understanding their lived experience.
- That professionals working with young people should have access to consistent resources, training, and adequate time to be able to deliver evidence-based interventions.
- Ensuring that the rights of the child are seen as the foundation for the development of any new policy decisions and curriculum design.
- Adopting an 'education first' approach to supporting young people around the risks associated with exchanging images, and speaking honestly about outcomes should the law need to be applied.

- That a legislative response to teenage sexting should mirror the support offered to adults; one that punishes those who coerce, extort, or non-consensually share images.

Final Words

Within this book the author has attempted to outline the epistemological grounding that underpins the theory of knowledge and issues around sexting across different academic disciplines. Moving then to identify an ontological approach that addresses, through a single theoretical framework, the existential conditions related to material, social, cultural contexts that sexting exists within as a means to gather and interpret both the quantitative and qualitative data produced from the research study. This has enabled the view of the participating boys as individuals but also identify a broader field of learning within the wider population of adolescent males in England, and act as a signpost to their corresponding behaviours. Utilising a positivistic enquiry approach with an attempt at interpretivism has allowed a degree of understanding of the teenage voice that exists alongside a clear legal and policy directive.

The scope of this book has not been about identifying an idiographic response to the 'truth' as experienced within a participant's individual situation, but rather to adopt a nomothetic approach that involves the study of different sub-sets of boys with the purpose of discovering the general principles or 'truths' that characterise the determinants, both individual and contextual, that lead to the practice of sexting amongst boys in general. It has been an important element within this book to reflect the voice of the teenage boys on the subject rather than solely the opinions of the academic professionals.

The book has attempted to shift perceived gendered double standard surrounding sexting and to move the narrative emphasis away from the sexual commodification of girls alone, who are held to greater account for their participation in sexting labelled as either identified victims or promiscuous, to the sexting behaviours of teenage boys in England. By developing these themes, a model of sexual citizenship based on the traditionally accepted standards of hegemonic heterosexual masculinity that subordinates other expressions of maleness can be challenged. Understanding the motivations that underpin teenage male sexting behaviour will help identify emotional openness and responsiveness within their development. It will also address the duality between a boy's own sexual experience and the expectations placed upon them within their social group. This new approach will allow practitioners supporting teenage boys to understand the motivational factors that prompt a sexting episode. Practitioners will then have access to more effective policy and strategy-based solutions that will allow them to determine the issues involved and arrive at a workable solution for intervention and support.

The theoretical construct of adolescence is difficult to define but must include the domains of social and cognitive psychology, and developmental neuroscience, each paradigm presenting theories that explore the development of the teenager. Whilst every teenager experiences an individual response to the biological, social, hormonal, and cultural changes that occur in growth and maturation, the theories of psychosocial development can view teenagers as a homogonous group and underestimate the variability of individual experience. If sexting is seen as a precursor to sexual activity, then the influence of pubertal development, and particularly the increase of sex hormones, needs to be recognised as a causal factor in sexting initiation rates. Concomitant causal links can be drawn between the physiological development of increasing testosterone levels, secondary sexual characteristics, and the psychological developments within adolescence as the main determinants and motivators to engage in sexual activity in teenage boys.

This study has revealed critical aspects that deserve further investigation, particularly the role pornography plays in sexting: the potential link to the Foucauldian assertion of the influence of biopower on the normalcy discourse and the social regulation of the physical body, and the possible links to a sense of entitlement felt by some boys around the collection and curation of naked images.

This book has sought to examine the sexting behaviours of boys aged 14 years to 18 years, including those whose sexual identity is recognised as 'other than heterosexual'. With the focus of the book being on peer-on-peer consensual sexting and where the intention to harm is not present; this is not to detract from the important recognition that pressure, coercion, or problematic gendered practices occur as factors within some sexting practice. Rather, to explore the motivations associated with the experimental sexting episodes that occur involving teenage boys.

Therefore, the axiology embedded within this approach has been to examine 'value' from a participant perspective, within the general, rather than a specific focus on moral or ethical values, and to emphasise the plurality and heterogeneity of the boys' experiences within the motivational factors expressed. The approach within this book has been one of resistance designed to ensure that alternative voices are not subsumed by an unquestioning adherence to the dominant 'harm' discourse.

To this end, it is appropriate to conclude with the thoughts around sexting by boys themselves:

> Well, I think of it [sexting] as portable intimacy, I'd say it's quite the cornerstone for a long-distance relationship, you know if you couldn't really contact them sometimes long distance it could just fizzle out. But now? It's social media and stuff. It's quite integral and so some of these relationships, as it is essentially you know it's on-line sex and it's a way for two people to be intimate when they're not together. (James, 17 years)

> It's quite normal actually [sexting], it normally only happens in a relationship between two people, but for random people to get sent nudes or exposed images it does happen. For example, say people are just trying to either mess about or their trying to what they call 'hit on' or try to get into relationship. (Steve, 16 years)

> I think it would be the same if I was gay or straight. I think people send images because they like you and you send back because you like them. It is about the person not the fact they are gay or straight, it is the person you like. It is about trust, if he sends you a picture it is because he trusts you, and if he sends you a picture it proves that he likes you. (Daniel, 14 years)

> If you feel like an outsider, and you can't find someone who is 'the person' for you then you are going to try to find people who accept you, need you and want you – you will look for that so that you can feel wanted and accepted by society. (James, 14 years)

> I think schools are out of touch with how young people feel about it, we aren't that bothered, it is all about personal choice. Schools should be reflecting this in how they teach things to keep us all safe. Schools just teach about heterosexual things; they need to reflect all of us in what they do. (John, 14 years)

Declaration

The author has no affiliations with or involvement in any organisation or entity with any financial interest. The study complied with ethical standards under the governance of the Research Ethics Committee of Newman University (PG2019/003).

All data was collected with the consent of the participants and the assent of their parents.

All names within the book have been anonymised.

No funding was provided for the study.

Adaption of the 'Motivational determinants of sexting' model by Sesar et al. (2019) made with permission.

References

Albury, K. (2017). Just because it's public doesn't mean it's any of your business: Adults' and children's sexual rights in digitally mediated spaces. *New Media & Society, 19*(5), 713–725.

Convention on the rights of the child. (1989). Treaty no. 27531. *United Nations Treaty Series*, 1577 (pp. 3–178). Accessed February 4, 2023, from https://treaties.un.org/doc/Treaties/1990/09/19900902%2003-14%20AM/Ch_IV_11p.pdf

Dodaj, A., & Sesar, K. (2020). Sexting categories. *Mediterranean Journal of Clinical Psychology, 8*, 2. Published online.

Elliott, I. A., Beech, A. R., & Mandeville-Norden, R. (2012). The psychological profiles of Internet, contact, and mixed internet/contact sex offenders. *Sexual Abuse, 25*(1), 3–20. https://doi.org/10.1177/1079063212439426 (Original work published 2013).

Great Britain. Department for Education. (2024). *Keeping children safe in education*. The Stationary Office.

Great Britain. Parliament. House of Commons All-Party Parliamentary Group. (2021). *Selfie generation: What's behind the rise of self-generated indecent images ofc children online?* The Stationary Office.

Hasinoff, A. (2015). *Sexting Panic: Rethinking criminalization, privacy, and consent* (p. 4). University of Illinois Press.

Hertlein, K., Shadid, C., & Steelman, S. (2015). Exploring perceptions of acceptability of sexting in same-sex, bisexual and heterosexual relationships, and communities. *Journal of Couple & Relationship Therapy, 14*(4), 342–357.

Hilton, Z., King, H., Curtis, L., Flessas, N., & O'Keefe-Dolby, C. (2024). *Shifting the dial: Methods to prevent 'self-generated' child sexual abuse among 11–13-year-olds*. Internet Matters.

Jørgensen, C., Weckesser, A., Turner, J., & Alex, W. (2018, June). Young people's views on sexting education and support needs: Findings and recommendations from a UK based study. *Sex Education: Sexuality, Society & Learning*, 1–19. Published Online.

Katz, A., & El Asam, A. (2019). *In their own words: The digital lives of schoolchildren*. Internet Matters.org, London.

Kloess, J. A., Woodhams, J., Whittle, H., Grant, T., & Hamilton-Giachritsis, C. E. (2019). The challenges of identifying and classifying child sexual abuse material. *Sexual Abuse, 31*(2), 173–196.

Needham, J. (2021). Sending nudes: Intent and risk associated with 'sexting' as understood by gay adolescent boys. *Sexuality & Culture, 5*(2), 396–416.

Ojeda, M., Del Rey, R., Ortega-Ruiz, R., & Casas, J. (2019). Sexting: A new way to explore sexuality. In F. Wright (Ed.), *Digital technology* (pp. 99–124). Nova Science.

Phippen, A., & Bond, E., 2023. A progressive future?. In *Policing teen sexting: Supporting children's rights while applying the law* (pp. 93–114). Springer International Publishing.

Reed, L., Boyer, M., Meskunas, H., Tolman, R., & Ward, M. (2020). How do adolescents experience sexting in dating relationships? Motivations to sext and responses to sexting requests from dating partners. *Children and Youth Services Review, 109*(104696), 1–10.

Sesar, K., Dodja, A., & Šimić, N. (2019). Motivational determinants of sexting: Towards a model of integrating the research. *Psihologijske Teme, 28*(3), 461–482.

Setty, E. (2019a). 'Confident' and 'hot' or 'desperate' and 'cowardly'? Meanings of young men's sexting practices in youth sexting culture. *Journal of Youth Studies*, Published on-line, July, 1–17.

Setty, E. (2019b). A rights-based approach to youth sexting: Challenging risk, shame, and the denial of rights to bodily and sexual expression within youth digital sexual culture. *International Journal of Bullying Prevention*, Published on-line, November 19, 1–14.

Walrave, M., Heirman, W., & Hallam, L. (2014). Under pressure to sext? Applying the theory of planned behaviour to adolescent sexting. *Behaviour & Information Technology, 33*(1), 85–97.

Wolak, J., & Finkelhor, D. (2011). *Sexting: A typology*. Crimes against Children Research Center. Published on-line, November, 1–16.

References

Ajzen, I. (2011). The theory of planned behaviour: Reactions and reflections. *Psychology & Health, 26*(9), 1113–1127.

Ajzen, I., Timko, C., & White, J. (1982). Self-monitoring and the attitude-behaviour relation. *Journal of Personality & Social Psychology, 42*(3), 426–435.

Ajzen, I., Timko, C., & White, J. (1991). The theory of planned behavior. *Organizational Behaviour and Human Decision Processes, 50*, 179–211.

Albury, K., & Byron, P. (2014). Queering sexting and sexualisation. *Media International Australia, 153*, 138–147.

Albury, K. (2015). Selfies, sexts, and sneaky hats: Young people's understandings of gendered practices of self-representation. *International Journal of Communication, 9*, 1734–1745.

Albury, K. (2017). Just because it's public doesn't mean it's any of your business: Adults' and children's sexual rights in digitally mediated spaces. *New Media & Society, 19*(5), 713–725.

Alipour, M. (2017). Essentialism and Islamic theology of homosexuality: A critical reflection on an essentialist epistemology toward same sex desires and acts in Islam. *Journal of Homosexuality, 64*(14), 1930–1942.

Anastassiou, A. (2017). Sexting and young people: A review of the qualitative literature. *The Qualitative Report, 22*(8), 2231–2239.

Anderson, E., & McCormack, M. (2018). Inclusive masculinity theory: Overview, reflection & refinement. *Journal of Gender Studies, 27*(5), 547–561.

Baker, N. (2024). *UK mobile phone statistics, 2024.* Accessed January 3, 2025, from https://www.uswitch.com/mobiles/studies/mobile-statistics/#uk-mobile-phone-user-statistics

© The Author(s), under exclusive license to Springer Nature Switzerland AG 2025
J. Needham, *Addressing Sexting in Educational Spaces*, Studies in Childhood and Youth,
https://doi.org/10.1007/978-3-031-96398-8

Bauermeister, J., Yeagley, E., Meanley, S., & Pingel, E. (2014). Sexting among young men who have sex with men: Results from a national survey. *Journal of Adolescent Health, 54,* 606–611.

Baumgartner, S., Valkenburg, P., & Peter, J. (2010). Assessing causality in relationship between adolescents' risky sexual online behaviour and their perceptions of this behaviour. *Journal of Youth Adolescence, 39,* 1226–1239.

Benotsch, E., Snipes, D., Martin, A., & Bull, S. (2013). Sexting, substance abuse and sexual risk behaviours in young adults. *Journal of Adolescent Health, 52,* 307–313.

Bianchi, D., Morelli, M., Baioco, R., & Chirumbolo, A. (2017). Sexting as a mirror on the wall: Body esteem attribution, media models and objectified body consciousness. *Journal of Adolescence, 61,* 164–172.

Bianchi, D., Baiocco, R., & Morelli, M. (2016). Psychometric properties of the sexting motivations questionnaire for adolescents and young adults. *Rassegna di Psicologia, 3*(35), 5–18.

Bianchi, D. Morelli, M. Baioco, R. Chirumbolo, A. (2019). Individual Differences and developmental trends in sexting motivations. *Current Psychology* Published on-line.

Bible, 1 Corinthians 6:18-19, Contemporary English Version.

Bible, Ephesians 5:3-4, Contemporary English Version.

Bible, Ezekiel 16:25, Contemporary English Version.

Bible, 1 Thessalonians 4: 3–7, Contemporary English Version.

Bragg, S., Ponsford, R., Meiksin, R., Emmerson, L., & Bonell, C. (2020). Dilemmas of school-based relationships and sexuality education for and about consent. *Sex Education: Sexuality, Society & Learning,* Published on-line June 1–15.

Burén, J., & Lunde, C. (2018). Sexting among adolescents: A nuanced and gendered online challenge for young people. *Computers in Human Behavior, 85,* 210–217.

Casas, J., Ojeda, M., Del Elipe, P., & Ray, R. (2019). Exploring which factors contribute to teens' participation in sexting. *Computers in Human Behavior, 100,* 60–69.

Cass, V. (1979). Homosexual identity formation, a theoretical model. *Journal of Homosexuality, 4*(3), 219–235.

Champion, A., & Pedersen, C. (2015). Investigating differences between sexters and non-sexters on attitudes, subjective norms, and risky sexual behaviours. *The Canadian Journal of Human Sexuality, 24*(3), 205–214.

Choi, H., Van Mori, C., Ouytsel, J., Madigan, S., & Temple, J. (2019). Adolescent sexting involvement over 4 years and associations with sexual activity. *Journal of Adolescent Health, 65,* 738–744.

CIBYL. (2021). *Growing up LGBT+.* Just Like Us.

Clancy, E., Klettke, B., Crossman, A., Hallford, D., Howard, D., & Toumbourou, J. (2021). Sext dissemination: Differences across nationals in motivation and associations. *International Journal of Environmental Research and Public Health, 18*(2429), 1–16.

Clarke, K., Cover, R., & Aggleton, P. (2018). Sex and ambivalence: LGBTQ youth negotiating sexual feelings, desires, and attractions. *Journal of LGBT Youth*, published online, June, 1–16.

Convention on the rights of the child. (1989). Treaty no. 27531. *United Nations Treaty Series*, 1577 (pp. 3–178). Accessed February 4, 2023, from https://treaties.un.org/doc/Treaties/1990/09/19900902%2003-14%20AM/Ch_IV_11p.pdf

Courtice, E., & Shaughnessy, K. (2017). Technology-mediated sexual interaction and relationships: A systematic review of the literature. *Sexual and Relationship Therapy, 32*(3–4), 269–290.

Davidson, J. (2014). *Sexting gender and teens.* Sense Publications.

de Gámez-Guadix, M., Santisteban, P., & Ressett, S. (2017). Sexting among Spanish adolescents: Prevalence and personality profiles. *Psicothema, 29*(1), 29–34.

De Kelley, N., & Santos, R. (2022). *Rainbow Britain—attraction, identity, and connection in Great Britain in 2022.* Stonewall.

Del Ray, R., Ojeda, M., Cassas, J., Mora-Merchán, J., & Elipe, P. (2019). Sexting among adolescents: The emotional impact and influence of the need for popularity. *Frontiers in Psychology, 10*(1828), 1–11.

Department for Education. (2019). *Relationships education, relationships, and sex education (RSE) and health education. Statutory guidance for governing bodies, proprietors, head teachers, principals, senior leadership teams, teachers.* HM Government.

Department for Education. (2020). National curriculum in England: science programmes of study. HM Government, [Online]. Accessed June 17, 2023, from https://www.gov.uk/government/publications/national-curriculum-in-england-science-programmes-of-study/national-curriculum-in-england-science-programmes-of-study

Dir, A., Coskunpina, A., Steiner, J., & Cynders, M. (2013). Understanding differences in sexting behaviours across gender, relationship status and sexual identity, and the role of expectancies in sexting. *Cyberpsychology Behavior, and Social Networking, 16*(8), 568–574.

Dodaj, A., & Sesar, K. (2020). Sexting categories. *Mediterranean Journal of Clinical Psychology, 8*, 2. Published online.

Drouin, M., & Chirumbolo, A. (2021). The relationship between dark triad personality traits and sexting behaviours among adolescents and young adults across 11 countries. *International Journal of Environmental Research and Public Health, 18*(2526), 1–25.

Dolev-Cohen, M., & Ricon, T. (2020). Demystifying sexting: Adolescent sexting and its associations with parenting styles and sense of parental control in Israel. *Cyberpsychology: Journal of Psychological Research on Cyberspace, 14*(6), 1–6.

Dolev-Cohen, M. (2024). Patterns of sexting by youths: A latent class analysis. *Journal of Sex & Marital Therapy, 50*(6), 679–690.

DeSousa, R. (2023). *A lot of it is actually just abuse. Young people and pornography'* Children's Commissioner.

Elliott, I. A., Beech, A. R., & Mandeville-Norden, R. (2012). The psychological profiles of Internet, contact, and mixed internet/contact sex offenders. *Sexual Abuse, 25*(1), 3–20. https://doi.org/10.1177/1079063212439426 (Original work published 2013).

El Katz, A., & Asam, A. (2019). *In their own words: The digital lives of schoolchildren.* Internet Matters.org.

Fairbairn, W. (1994). Theoretical contributions to Object relations theory. In D. Shariff & E. Fairbairn-Birtles (Eds.), *From instinct to self; Selected papers of WRD Fairbairn, Volume 1 Clinical and theoretical papers* (pp. 200–264). E-book 2021, International Psychology Institute.

Foody, M., Kuldas, S., Sargioti, A., Mazzone A., & O'Higgins Norman, J. (2023). Sexting behaviour among adolescents: Do friendship quality and social competence matter? *Computers in Human Behavior, 142*, 1–8. ISSN 0747-5632.

Foody, M., Mazzone, A., Laffan, D., Loftsson, M., & O'Higgins-Norman, J. (2021). It's not just sexy pics' An investigation into sexting behaviour and behavioural problems in adolescents. *Computers in Human Behavior, 117*(106662), 1–8.

García-Gómez, A. (2019). Sexting and hegemonic masculinity: Interrogating male sexual agency. In P. Bou-Franch & B. Garecés-Conejos (Eds.), *Empowerment and Dominant Gendered Norms: New Insights and Future Directions* (pp. 313–339). Analyzing Digital Discourse.

Gassó, M., Klettke, B., Agustina, J., & Montiel, I. (2019). Sexting, mental health, and victimisation among adolescents: A literature review. *International Journal of Environmental Research and Public Health, 16*, 1–14.

Gilligan, C. (1977). In a different voice: Women's conceptions of self and morality. *Harvard Educational Review, 47*, 481–517.

Glascow, P. (2005). *Fundamentals of survey research methodology.* MITRE, Washington C3 Centre, McLean, Virginia (I - 2-5).

Great Britain. Parliament. House of Commons All-Party Parliamentary Group. (2021). *Selfie generation: What's behind the rise of self-generated indecent images ofc children online?* The Stationary Office.

Great Britain. Parliament. House of Commons. (2022). *On-line safety bill.* The Stationary Office.

Great Britain. Government Equalities Office. (2023). *National LGBT Survey.* The Stationary Office.

Great Britain. Department for Education. (2024). *Keeping children safe in education*. The Stationary Office.

Hackett, P. (2019). *Harmful sexual behaviour framework* (2nd ed.). NSPCC, UK. [online] Accessed 25/04/23, from https://www.icmec.org/wp-content/uploads/2019/04/harmful-sexual-behaviour-framework.pdf

Hadley, J. (1989). The neurobiology of motivational systems. In J. Lichtenberg (Ed.), *Psychoanalysis and motivation*. The Analytic Press.

Hammack, L., & Manago, M. (2024). The psychology of sexual and gender diversity in the 21st century: Social technologies and stories of authenticity. *American Psychologist*. Advance online publication. https://doi.org/10.1037/amp0001366

Hasinoff, A. (2015). *Sexting Panic: Rethinking criminalization, privacy, and consent* (p. 4). University of Illinois Press.

Hertlein, K., Shadid, C., & Steelman, S. (2015). Exploring perceptions of acceptability of sexting in same-sex, bisexual and heterosexual relationships, and communities. *Journal of Couple & Relationship Therapy, 14*(4), 342–357.

Hilton, Z., King, H., Curtis, L., Flessas, N., & O'Keefe-Dolby, C. (2024). *Shifting the dial: Methods to prevent 'self-generated' child sexual abuse among 11–13-year-olds*. Internet Matters.

Holt, T., Bossler, A., Malinski, R., & May, D. (2016). Identifying predictors of unwanted online sexual conversations among youth using a low self-control and routine activity framework. *Journal of Contemporary Criminal Justice, 32*(2), 108–128.

Holoyda, B., Landess, J., Sorrentino, R., & Hatters-Friedman, S. (2018). Trouble at teens fingertips: Youth sexting and the law. *Behavioural Science Law, 36*, 170–181.

Houck, C., Barker, D., Rizzo, C., Hancock, E., Norton, A., & Brown, L. (2014). Sexting and sexual behaviour in at-risk adolescents. *Pediatrics, 133*(2), e276–e282.

Hughes-Nind, J., & Braig, L. (2023). *Measuring online harms exposure among children* (pp. 1–39). Social Finance.

Ico.org.uk. (2018). *Guide to the UK General Data Protection Regulation (UK GDPR)*. [online] Accessed 01/01/23, from <https://ico.org.uk/for-organisations/guide-to-data-protection/guide-to-the-general-data-protection-regulation-gdpr/

Jacobson, R., & Joel, D. (2019). Self-reported gender identity and sexuality in an on-line sample of cisgender, transgender, and gender diverse individuals: An exploratory study. *The Journal of Sex Research, 56*(2), 249–263.

Jacobson, L., Daire, A., Abel, E., & Lambie, G. (2015). Gender expressions differences in same-sex intimate partner violence victimization, perpetration, and attitudes among LGBTQ college students. *Journal of LGBT Issues in Counselling, 9*, 199–216.

Jonsson, L., Bladh, M., Priebe, G., & Svedin, C. (2015). Online sexual behaviours among Swedish youth: Associations to background factors, behaviours, and abuse. *European Child and Adolescent Psychiatry, 24*, 1245–1260.

Jørgensen, C., Weckesser, A., Turner, J., & Alex, W. (2018, June). Young people's views on sexting education and support needs: Findings and recommendations from a UK based study. *Sex Education: Sexuality, Society & Learning*, 1–19. Published Online.

Katz, A., & El Asam, A. (2019). *In their own words: The digital lives of schoolchildren*. Internet Matters.org, London.

Kernsmith, P., Victor, B., & Smith-Darden, J. (2018). Online, offline, and over the line: Coercive sexting among adolescent dating partners. *Youth & Society, 50*(2), 1–14.

Kloess, J. A., Woodhams, J., Whittle, H., Grant, T., & Hamilton-Giachritsis, C. E. (2019). The challenges of identifying and classifying child sexual abuse material. *Sexual Abuse, 31*(2), 173–196.

Kolano, M. (2013). *Subject-relating and object-relating: An intersubjective exploration of adolescent texting*. PhD Dissertation, Chicago School of Professional Psychology.

Korenis, P., & Billick, S. (2014). Forensic implications: Adolescent sexting and cyberbullying. *Psychiatry, 85*, 97–101.

Kosenko, K., Luurs, G., & Binder, A. (2017). Sexting and sexual behaviour, 2011-2015: A critical review and meta-analysis of growing literature. *Computer-Mediated Communication, 22*, 141–160.

Kosciw, J., Palmer, N., & Kull, R. (2015). Reflecting resiliency: Openness about sexual orientation and/or gender identity and its relationship to well-being and educational outcomes for LGBT students. *American Journal of Community Psychology, 55*, 167–178.

La Handschuh, C., Cross, A., & Smaldone, A. (2018). Is sexting associated with sexual behaviours during adolescence? A systematic literature review and meta-analysis. *Journal of Midwifery & Women's Health, 64*(1), 88–97.

Lee, M., & Crofts, T. (2015). Gender, pressure, coercion, and pleasure: Untangling motivations for sexting between young people. *British Journal of Criminology, 55*, 454–473.

Lee, N., & Noor, Z. (2016). Islam or progress of the nation: An assessment of the aurat issue in Malay newspapers and magazines in the 1930s. *Malaysian Journal of Society and Space, 12*(6), 43–50.

Lee, M., & Rosenthal, S. (2023). Gender-affirming care of transgender and gender-diverse youth: Current concepts. *Annual Review Medicine, 74*, 107–116.

Lichtenberg, J. (2013). *Psychoanalysis and motivation*. The Analytic Press.

Lindquist, A., Sendén, M., & Renström, E. (2021). What is gender, anyway: A review of the options for operationalising gender. *Psychology & Sexuality, 12*(4), 332–344.

Lippman, M., Lawlor, N., & Leistner, C. (2023). Learning on onlyfans: User perspectives on knowledge and skills acquired on the platform. *Journal of Sex and Sexuality, 27,* 1203–1223.

Livingstone, S., & Smith, P. (2014). Annual research review: Harms experienced by child users of online and mobile technologies: The nature, prevalence, and management of sexual and aggressive risks in the digital age. *Journal of Child Psychology and Psychiatry, 55*(6), 635–654.

Maes, C., & Vandenbosch, L. (2022). Physically distant, virtually close: Adolescents' sexting behaviors during a strict lockdown period of the COVID-19 pandemic. *Computers in Human Behavior, 126,* 1–12.

Maheux, A., Evans, R., Widman, L., Nesi, J., Prinstein, M., & Choukas-Bradley, S. (2020). Popular peer norms and adolescent sexting behaviour. *Journal of Adolescence, 78,* 62–66.

Martel, M. (2013). Sexual selection and sex differences in the prevalence of childhood and adolescent internalizing disorders. *Psychological Bulletin, 139*(6), 1221–1259.

Mayo, C. (2022). Gender diversities and sex education. *Journal of Philosophy of Education, 10*(1111), 1467–9752.

McKie, R., Milhausen, R., & Lachowsky, N. (2016). Hedge you bets': Technology's role in young gay men's relationship challenges. *Journal of Homosexuality,* Published on-line, April, 1–20.

McCormack, M. (2011). Mapping the terrain of homosexually themed language. *British Journal of Sociology, 58*(5), 1664–1679.

McConnell, E., Clifford, A., Korpak, A., Phillips, G., II, & Birkett, M. (2017). Identity, victimisation, and support: Facebook experiences and mental health among LGBTQ youth. *Computer Human Behaviour, 76,* 237–244.

Medrano, J., Rosales, F., & Gámez-Guadix, M. (2018). Assessing the links of sexting, cybervictimization, depression, and suicidal ideation among university students. *Archives of Suicide Research, 22,* 153–164.

Mohammad, T., & Nooraini, I. (2021). Routine activity theory and juvenile delinquency: The roles of peers and family monitoring among Malaysian adolescents. *Children and Youth Services Review, 121*(C), 105795.

Morelli, M., Urbini, F., Bianchi, D., Baiocco, R., Cattelino, E., Laghi, F., Sorokowski, P., Misiak, M., Dziekan, M., Hudson, H., Marshall, A., Nguyen, T., Mark, L., Kopecky, K., Szotkowski, R., Van Demirtaş, E., Outsel, J., Voiskounsky, A., Bogacheva, N., Ioannou, M., Synott, J., Tzani-Pepelasi, K., Balakrishnan, V., Okumu, M., Small, E., Nikolova, S., Drouin, M., & Chirumbolo, A. (2021). The relationship between dark triad personality traits and sexting behaviours among adolescents and young adults across 11 countries. *International Journal of Environmental Research and Public Health, 18*(2526), 1–25.

Motschenbacher, H. (2011). Taking queer linguistics further: Sociolinguistics and critical heteronormativity research. *International Journal of Social Language, 212*, 149–179.

Mowlabocus, S. (2007). Gay men and the pornification of everyday life. In S. Paasonen, K. Nikunen, & L. Soarenmaa (Eds.), *Pornification: Sex and sexuality in media culture* (pp. 61–71). Berg.

Muss, R., Velder, E., & Porton, H. (1996). *Theories of adolescence* (6th ed.). McGraw-Hill.

Naezer, M. (2018). From risky behaviour to sexy adventures: Reconceptualising young people's online sexual activities. *Culture, Health & Sexuality, 20*(6), 715–729.

Needham, J. (2021). Sending nudes: Intent and risk associated with 'sexting' as understood by gay adolescent boys. *Sexuality & Culture, 5*(2), 396–416.

Office for National Statistics. (2021). Accessed 01/05/2023, from https://www.ons.gov.uk/datasets/TS030/editions/2021/versions/3

Office for National Statistics. (2022). Accessed 06/02/23, from https://explore-education-statistics.service.gov.uk/data-tables/fast-track/fdf8e3d7-4420-441d-8084-6a8d82ff4bea

Office for National Statistics. (2023). Accessed 03/04/23, from https://www.ons.gov.uk/datasets/TS078/editions/2021/versions/2/filter-outputs/f7947ae3-266e-4e76-be6f-85a0564b8337#get-data

Ojeda, M., Del Rey, R., Ortega-Ruiz, R., & Casas, J. (2019). Sexting: A new way to explore sexuality. In F. Wright (Ed.), *Digital technology* (pp. 99–124). Nova Science.

O'Sullivan, L. (2014). Linking online sexual activities to health outcomes among teens'. *New Directions for Child and Adolescent Development, 144*, 37–51.

Oyetunji, Y (2022). *Pornography viewing predictors among secondary school adolescents in Illinois, Chicago.* Accessed Jun 21, 2023, from https://www.researchgate.net/publication/362479179_PORNOGRAPHY_VIEWING_PREDICTORS_AMONG_SECONDARY_SCHOOL_ADOLESCENTS_IN_ILLINOIS_CHICAGO

Paasonen, S. Light, B., & Jarrett, K. (2019). The dic pic: Harassment, curation, and desire. *Social Media and Society*, April–June, 1–10.

Patchin, J., & Hinduja, S. (2020). It is time to teach safe sexting? *Journal of Adolescent Health, 66*, 140–143.

Phippen, A., & Brennan, M. (2016). The new normal? *Young People, Technology & Online Behaviour.* Accessed March 3, 2023, from https://www.nota.co.uk/

Phippen, A., & Bond, E., 2023. A progressive future?. In *Policing teen sexting: Supporting children's rights while applying the law* (pp. 93–114). Springer International Publishing.

Pingle, J., Mills, K., McAteer, J., Jepson, R., Hogg, E., Anand, N., & Blakemore, S. (2018). The physiology of adolescent sexual behaviour: A systematic review. *Cogent Social Sciences, 3*, 1–14.

Pylypa, J. (1998). Power and bodily practice: Applying the work of Foucault to an anthropology of the body. *Arizona Anthropologist, 13*, 21–36.

Qur'ān. (2012a). Sūrah al-Isra 17: 18.

Qur'ān. (2012b). Sūrah An-Nur, 24:30-31.

Qur'ān. (2012c). Sūrah at-Tawbah, 9:108.

Race, K. (2007). The use of pleasure in harm reduction: Perspectives from the history of sexuality. *International Journal of Drug Policy, 715*, 1–7.

Raine, G., Khouja, C., Scott, R., Wright, K., & Sowden, A. (2020). Pornography use and sexting amongst children and young people: A systematic overview of reviews. *Systematic Reviews, 9*(283), 1–12.

Reed, L., Boyer, M., Meskunas, H., Tolman, R., & Ward, M. (2020). How do adolescents experience sexting in dating relationships? Motivations to sext and responses to sexting requests from dating partners. *Children and Youth Services Review, 109*(104696), 1–10.

Rentería, R., Feinstein, B., Dyar, C., & Watson, R. (2023). Does outness function the same for all sexual minority youth? Testing its associations with different aspects of well-being in a sample of youth with diverse sexual identities. *Psychology Sex Orientation Gender Diversity, 10*(3), 490–497.

Ricciardelli, R., & Adorjan, M. (2018). If a girl's photo gets sent around, that's a way bigger deal than if a guy's photo gets sent around: Gender, sexting, and the teenage years. *Journal of Gender Studies, 28*(5), 563–577.

Rice, E., Gibbs, J., Winetrobe, H., Rhoades, H., Plant, A., Montoya, J., & Kordic, T. (2014). Sexting behavior among middle school students. *Pediatrics, 134*(1), e21–e28.

Rosen, N. Peralta, R., & Merrill, M. (2019). Learning how sexual minorities in school and at home: How critical pedagogy can challenge heterosexism. *Cogent Education*.

Ryan, G., Schubert, A., & Wurf, G. (2014). Adolescent setting in schools: Criminalisation, policy imperatives, and duty of care. *Issues in Educational Research, 24*(2), 190–211.

Sagrera, C., Magner, J., Temple, J., Lawrence, R., Magner, T., Avila-Quintero, V., McPherson, P., Alderman, L., Bhuiyan, M., Patterson, J., & Murnane, K. (2022). Social media use and body image issues among adolescents in a vulnerable Louisiana community. *Front Psychiatry, 13*, 1–14.

Ševcíková, A. (2016). Girl' and boys' experience with teen sexting in early and late adolescence. *Journal of Adolescence, 51*, 156–162.

Sesar, K., Dodja, A., & Šimić, N. (2019). Motivational determinants of sexting: Towards a model of integrating the research. *Psihologijske Teme, 28*(3), 461–482.

Skoog, T., Sorbring, E., Hallberg, J., & Bohlin, M. (2013). Boy's pubertal timing measured on the pubertal development scales linked to online sexual activities. *International Journal of Sexual Health, 25,* 281–290.

Setty, E. (2019a). 'Confident' and 'hot' or 'desperate' and 'cowardly'? Meanings of young men's sexting practices in youth sexting culture. *Journal of Youth Studies,* Published on-line, July, 1–17.

Setty, E. (2019b). A rights-based approach to youth sexting: Challenging risk, shame, and the denial of rights to bodily and sexual expression within youth digital sexual culture. *International Journal of Bullying Prevention,* Published on-line, November 19, 1–14.

Setty, E. (2020). *Risk & harm in youth sexting culture – young people's perspectives.* Routledge.

Setty, E. (2021). Speaking the unspeakable: Education about youth digital intimacies in schools. *Academia Letters,* Article 483.

Setty, E., Ringrose, J., & Hunt, J. (2024). From 'harmful sexual behaviour' to 'harmful sexual culture': Addressing school-related sexual and gender-based violence among young people in England through 'post-digital sexual citizenship'. *Gender and Education, 36*(5), 434–452.

Sheilds Dobson, A., & Ringrose, J. (2016). Sext education: Pedagogies of sex, gender, and shame in schoolyards of tagged and exposed. *Sex Education: Sexuality, Society & Learning, 6*(1), 8–21.

Statista Smartphone ownership penetration. (2023). Accessed January 07, 2023, from https://www.statista.com/statistics/271851/smartphone-owners-in-the-united-kingdom-uk-by-age/

Stanley, N., Barter, C., Wood, M., Aghtaie, N., Larkins, C., Lanau, A., & Överlien, C. (2018). Pornography, sexual coercion and abuse and sexting in young people's intimate relationships: A European study. *Journal of Interpersonal Violence, 33*(19), 2919–2944.

Steinberg, L. (2010). Commentary: A behavioural scientist looks at the science of adolescent brain development. *Brain and Cognition, 72*(1), 60–164.

Symons, K., Ponnet, K., Walrave, M., & Heirman, W. (2018). Sexting scripts in adolescent relationships: Is sexting becoming the norm? *New Media & Society, 20*(10), 3839–3857.

Suler, J. (2004). The online disinhibition effect. *Cyberpsychology & Behavior, 7*(3), 321–326.

Talmud. Sanhedrin 75a:2.

Talmud. Nedarim 20a:11.

Temple, J., & Choi, H. (2014). Longitudinal association between teen sexting and sexual behaviour. *Pediatrics, 134*(5), e1287–e1292.

Turvey, B., & Freeman, J. (2014). *Victim lifestyle exposure.* In B. Turvey (Ed.), *Forensic victimology* (2nd ed., pp. 143–176). Academic.

UK Council for Internet Safety. (2020). Sharing nudes and semi-nudes Advice for education settings working with children and young people Responding to incidents and safeguarding children and young people. UK Council for Internet Safety.

UN Human Rights Council, *Optional Protocol to the Convention on the Rights of the Child on a Communications Procedure: resolution / adopted by the Human Rights Council*, 14 July 2011, A/HRC/RES/17/18. Accessed June 17, 2023, from https://www.refworld.org/docid/4e72fbb12.html

Unis, B., & Sällström, C. (2019). 'Adolescents' conceptions of learning and education about sex and relationships. *American Journal of Sexuality Education*, Published On-line, June, 1–28.

Van Dijke, S., Van den Eynde, S., & Enzlin, P. (2025). The bright side of sexting: A scoping review on its benefits. *Computers in Human Behavior, 164*, 108499. https://doi.org/10.1016/j.chb.2024.108499

Van Ouytsel, J., & Dhoest, A. (2021). The prevalence, context, and perceptions of sexting among non-heterosexual men from various generations in Belgium. *Computers in Human Behavior, 126*. Published on-line.

Van Ouytsel, J., Ponnet, K., & Walrave, M. (2014). The associations between adolescents' consumption of pornography and music videos and their sexting behavior. *Cyberpsychology, Behavior and Social Networking, 17*(12), 772–778.

Van Ouytsel, J., Walrave, M., Ponnet, K., & Heirman, W. (2015). The association between adolescent sexting, psychosocial difficulties and risk behavior: Integrative review. *The Journal of School Nursing, 31*(1), 54–69.

Van Ouytsel, J., Van Gool, E., Walrave, M., Ponnet, K., & Peeters, E. (2016). Exploring the role of social networking sites within adolescent romantic relationships and dating experiences. *Computers in Human Behavior, 55*, 76–86.

Van Oosten, J., & Vandenbosch, L. (2017). Sexy online self-presentation on social network sites and the willingness to engage in sexting: A comparison of gender and age. *Journal of Adolescence, 54*, 42–50.

Velázquez, J. (2023). Feeling in values: Axiological and emotional intentionality as living structure of ethical life, regarding Max Scheler's phenomenology. *Human Studies, 46*, 43–57.

Waling, A., & Pym, T. (2017). C'mon, no one wants a dic pic: Exploring the cultural framings of the dic pic in contemporary online publics. *Journal of Gender Studies, 28*, 70.

Walrave, M., Heirman, W., & Hallam, L. (2014). Under pressure to sext? Applying the theory of planned behaviour to adolescent sexting. *Behaviour & Information Technology, 33*(1), 85–97.

Weisskirch, R., Drouin, M., & Delevi, R. (2017). Relational anxiety and sexting. *The Journal of Sex Research, 54*(6), 685–693.

Wolak, J., & Finkelhor, D. (2011). *Sexting: A typology.* Crimes against Children Research Center. Published on-line, November, 1–16.

YouGov Survey Mobile Phone Ownership. (2019). Accessed January 07, 2023, from https://docs.cdn.yougov.com/kp1bpgx43s/YouGov%20-%20Kids%20and%20tech%20Results.pdf

Yunkaporta, T., & Shillingsworth, D. (2020). Relationally responsive standpoint. *Journal of Indigenous Research, 8*(4), 1–14.

Index

A
Abrahamic religions, 65, 67, 73
Active sexting, 2, 3, 54, 55, 57, 61–63, 67–73, 78, 83, 84, 86, 88–91, 96, 98–100, 109, 112, 114
Adolescence (Western construct), 24
Adolescents
  brain development, 25, 26, 29
  development, 14, 16, 17, 129
  identity, 30, 31, 36
  risk-taking, 30, 42
  sexting, 12, 16, 17
Affirmation, 86
Age and sexting, 55, 62, 63, 130, 133
Agency (sexual), 24–27
Age of consent, 125, 134, 135
Age range, 49, 51
Aggravated sexting, 110, 111, 115, 145, 149
Aggregated data, 48
AI-generated images, 2
Analysis blocks, 50
Androcentric theories, 29

Apostasy, 66, 131
Arousal, 98–100, 115
Asian British heritage, 70
Associated risks, 24, 36–42
Atheism, 49, 67, 69, 73
Attitudes and expectations, 50
Attitudes toward sexting, 15
Attraction, 103
Autonomy, 17
Avoidance of punishment, 17
Axiological approach, 127
Axiology, 6, 48, 153

B
Behavioural change, 34
Behavioural control, 14–17
Behavioural disposition, 14
Behavioural norms, 19, 106, 133
Behavioural reinforcement, 19, 34
Behavioural traits, 3
Behaviour policy, 144
Biological development, 29
Bisexuality, 82

Boarding schools, 71–74
Body image, 19, 30, 96, 101–106, 115, 121, 141, 145
Body positivity, 4
Body self-esteem, 101
Boys' experiences, 7, 153
Boys' relationships, 63, 71
Bronfenbrenner's Ecological Systems Theory, 35

C
Capable guardians, 72
Capable guardianship, 35
Cass, homosexual identity formation, 28
Casual sex, 87
Categorical classification, 2
Census sampling, 48
Child protection, 144, 145, 150
Christianity, 65, 66, 68, 69, 73
Clustered population, 48
Coercion, 5, 6, 112, 113, 120, 124, 135, 142, 148, 150, 153
Cognitive development, 16, 24, 33–36
Cognitive psychology, 25
Cohorts, 48, 49, 51
Coming out, 80–82
Communication technology, 2
Community belonging, 86
Comparative generalisation, 50
Conceptual framework, 12, 14–17
Conceptual limitations, 2
Consent, 2, 4, 146, 150, 155
Contextual determinants, 18
Criterion measurement, 48
Cultural conditioning, 34
Cultural determinants, 54–74
Cultural hegemony, 123
Cultural relativism, 24
Cultural shift, 79
Cultural values, 18

Curated images, 3, 19, 108
Curriculum delivery, 143, 149–152
Curriculum development, 121–124

D
Data collection, 48
Data protection (GDPR), 134
Definitions of sexting, 2–3, 5
Delinquent behaviour, 18
Delinquent peers, 42
Demographic characteristics, 17
Demographic factors, 124
Dependent variables, 48
Desire and power, 78
Developmental neuroscience, 25
Deviancy framework, 149
Digital communication, 13–14
Digital media platforms, 2
Digital platforms, 14, 26, 65
Digital rights, 147
Digital sexual ethics, 123
Disclosure (sexual identity), 28, 81, 88
Discomfort with sexts, 98–102, 104–106, 112, 115
Disinhibition, 84
Dominance, 17
Double standards, 5, 6, 37
Dual heritage, 70
Dyadic satisfaction, 110

E
Emotional health, 125
Emotional openness, 88, 152
Emotional regulation, 30
Emotional well-being, 103
Epistemology, 12
Equity effects, 50
Erikson's Psychosocial Theory, 31
Erotic content, 2
Ethical objections, 115

INDEX 171

Ethical reasoning, 34
Ethical values, 6, 7
Ethnic groups, 49
Ethnicity, 70–71
Ethnicity and sexting, 70, 71, 126
Ethnocentrism, 24
Excitement and novelty, 17
Executive functioning, 25
Experimental sexting, 2, 5, 41, 42, 123, 134, 141, 145, 147–150, 153
Explanatory variables, 50
Explicit content, 54, 62, 64
Exploitation, 96, 111–115
Exposure to sexting, 54

F
Fairbairn (1944) – Object Relations Theory, 31
Faith and sexting, 18, 63–68, 126
Faith structure, 49
Fantasy vs. reality, 83
Findings validation, 48
Flirting, 15, 19, 96–116, 141, 142
Foucauldian theory, 78
Foucault, Michel, 78
  biopower, 129
  sexuality, 26, 28, 30, 31, 36
Four Motivations Options Typology for Boys (4MOTB), 146, 149
Frameworks for motivation, 16
Frameworks for sexting, 5
Freedom of expression, 148
Freud's Psychosexual Development, 30

G
Gay community, 85–87
Gendered double standard, 5
Gender diverse, 78–80, 82, 83, 90
Gender expression, 79

Gender identity, 6, 14, 24, 27, 28, 31, 56, 58, 78, 79, 120, 122, 127, 128
General discussion, 119–135
Generalisation, 50
Geospatial applications, 12
Group bonding, 108
Guardianship, 33–36
Guidance for schools, 140, 141, 145

H
Harm discourse, 7
Harmful behaviour, 111, 112
Harm reduction, 15, 142, 150–152
Hegemonic masculinity, 3, 5
Heterogeneity, 50
Heteronormativity, 122, 123, 130
Heuristics, 31
Heuristic Stages (Sullivan), 31
Hill's Context-Based Model, 36
Humour and banter, 108, 109

I
Identity confusion, 31
Identity development, 125
Identity formation, 19, 28, 29
Identity management, 80
Image content, 103, 104
Images
  AI-generated, 2
  explicit, 2–4
  suggestive, 2
Impulse control, 17
Impulsivity, 42
Inclusion, 39, 122
Inclusion strategy, 143, 149
Independent variables, 48
Individual constructions, 6
Individual determinants, 16
Initiation age, 73

Intent to harm, 5
Interpretation of sexting, 14, 16
Interpretivism, 6, 51
Intersectionality, 120
Interviews (semi-structured), 50
Intimacy, 14, 30–32, 34, 39, 97–101, 133, 141, 149, 154
Intimate relationships, 88–89, 91
Islam, 63–65, 67, 68, 73

J
Joke images, 3
Joke sexting, 108
Judaism, 64, 65, 69, 73
Justification of behaviour, 15

K
Kohlberg's moral development, 32

L
Law and sexting, 12
Legal age to sext, 134–135
Legal majority, 12
Legal reform, 146, 147, 149–151
LGBTQ+ youth, 80
Limbic system, 25
Lived experience, 5, 121, 123, 142, 145, 151
Lust dynamism, 31

M
Malicious sexting, 2
Masculinity, 19, 88, 102, 108, 120, 125, 142, 143, 152
Masturbatory aid, 62
Mead (1950) – Cultural Conditioning, 32
Mesosystem, 35
Methodological strategy, 50

Mobile phone access, 54
Moral crisis, 5
Moral development, 32
Motivated offenders, 72, 73
Motivation, 4–7
Motivational determinants model, 16–20, 50
Motivation to sext, 18, 19, 29, 30, 96–97, 113, 141–144

N
Neurodevelopment, 25
Nomothetic approach, 6
Normal adolescent behaviour, 112
Normative behaviour, 5, 140
Normative influences, 15

O
Object relations, 31
On-line harm, 121
On-line persona, 81
On-line sexual behaviour, 40
On-line vulnerability, 42
OnlyFans, 123
Ontology, 12
Ordinal variables, 49
Outness, 80, 81

P
Parental consent, 134
Participant voice, 6
Passion, 98, 100–101, 110, 115
Passive sexting, 2, 3, 54–58, 67, 70
Pastoral support, 140, 149
Peer feedback, 19
Peer influence, 25, 35
Peer norms, 107, 132
Peer pressure, 4, 16
Peer relationships, 30
Perceived behavioural control, 15–17

Personal attitudes, 14
Personal, Social, Health Education (PHSE), 143
Phenomenological interpretation, 51
Photo-sharing, 85
Piaget, 32
Planned Behaviour Theory, 14–17
Pleasure and subjectivity, 78
Pleasure-seeking, 17
Policy design, 5
Policy development, 13, 144–145
Pornographic content, 3
Pornography, 18, 39, 40, 54, 59–63, 104, 105, 121, 124, 129, 130, 133, 143, 148, 153
Power dynamics, 17
Pragmatic approach, 51
Predictive validity, 48
Pre-frontal cortex, 25
Pressure to sext, 84
Privacy, 85, 121, 148
Protectionist approach, 18
Psychological development, 15
Psychosocial development, 25, 29–34
Pubertal development, 54, 55, 59
Puberty, 29, 36
Public *vs.* private selfies, 3, 107
Pupil safeguarding, 141, 144–146

Q
Qualitative data, 50
Quantitative data, 48, 50
Queer community ethics, 108
Queer identity, 80
Questionnaire, 48, 50, 51

R
Region-based sampling, 49
Relationship education, 140–142, 145
Relationships, 57, 60–64, 68–74
Relationship scripts, 97, 149

Relationship status, 18, 124
Reliability, 50
Religion, 49
Religious identity, 67
Reputational harm, 27, 42
Rights-based approach, 146–148
Rights-based education, 146–148
Risk and benefit, 24, 36–42
Risk mitigation, 143
Risk-taking, 90
Risk-taking behaviour, 30, 42, 125
Romantic relationships, 97, 100
Routine Activity Theory, 35, 72

S
Safeguarding, 35, 54, 141, 144–146
Safe-sex curriculum, 122
Sample boosts, 50
Sampling plan, 48
School context, 50
School designation, 71–73
School engagement, 51
School ethos, 28
School inclusion, 143–145, 149
School policy, 145
Scopophilia, 58
Secondary sexual characteristics, 101, 102
Self-disclosure, 39, 134
Self-esteem, 28, 29
Self-expression, 89, 131, 134, 147–149
Self-generated content, 2–4
Self-image, 4, 141
Self-reflection, 33
Selman's Social Cognition Model, 32, 33
Semantics of sexting, 4
Sexting and identity, 78–83
Sexting and relationships, 87–89
Sexting content, 56–59
Sexting legislation, 134

Sexting rates, 54–55, 61, 70, 71, 73, 74
Sexting typologies, 140
Sexual agency, 14, 110, 121, 123, 133, 144
Sexual arousal, 98–100
Sexual availability, 85
Sexual citizenship, 5, 26, 152
Sexual content, 2
Sexual development, 30, 31
Sexual expression, 5, 6, 18, 96–113
Sexual identity, 17, 19, 27–29, 31, 39, 49, 50, 56, 57, 62, 63, 69, 78–88, 108, 127, 128, 131, 134, 153
Sexualised behaviour, 5
Sexual literacy, 123
Sexual minorities, 81, 86
Sexual motivation, 12, 14, 16, 17, 115
Sexual orientation, 27, 28, 78–80, 83, 87, 90, 91
Sexual risk, 38
Smartphone ownership, 54
Social acceptance, 87
Social Cognitive Theory, 34, 40
Social cohesion, 19, 120, 142
Social determinants, 74
Social learning, 34
Social learning theory, 16
Social media, 12, 19, 40, 41, 54, 84, 101, 102, 105, 107, 154
Social norms, 4, 17, 85
Social status, 96–116, 133
Societal expectations, 16, 30, 40
Sociocultural context, 19
Statutory framework, 140, 149
Stigma, 42
Stranger sexting, 69
Stratified sampling, 48, 50
Sub-categories of motivation, 105, 108
Sub-cultures, 3, 5, 125
Subjective judgement, 145
Subjective norms, 14–17

Subjectivity, 121
Suitable targets, 72, 73
Support strategies, 142, 145
Survey design, 49

T
Taxonomies of identity, 79
Technological access, 13, 15
Technology access, 73
Technology-mediated interaction, 3
Teenage boys, 12, 15
Teenage sexuality, 130, 146
Testosterone, 25, 29
Theory of Planned Behaviour, 14–17
Thorarche, 25, 55
Transgender youth, 83
Trauma-informed response, 121
Trend analysis, 69
Triangulation, 50
Trust, 39, 97, 101, 108, 109, 154
Typology model, 2–8, 12, 140, 141, 144, 147, 149

U
UK law, 12
Unconscious motivation, 18
Unintended consequences, 34, 36–38, 42

V
Validation, 15
Validity, 48, 50
Values, 6, 7, 14, 18
Variables
  dependent, 48
  independent, 48
Victim blaming, 123, 135
Viewing of pornography, 50
Voice of the participant, 6, 91
Vulnerability, 35, 42, 125

GPSR Compliance

The European Union's (EU) General Product Safety Regulation (GPSR) is a set of rules that requires consumer products to be safe and our obligations to ensure this.

If you have any concerns about our products, you can contact us on

ProductSafety@springernature.com

In case Publisher is established outside the EU, the EU authorized representative is:

Springer Nature Customer Service Center GmbH
Europaplatz 3
69115 Heidelberg, Germany

www.ingramcontent.com/pod-product-compliance
Ingram Content Group UK Ltd.
Pitfield, Milton Keynes, MK11 3LW, UK
UKHW042016040925

462589UK00004B/13